To my husband,
Joe

QUILTING
1915-1983

An Annotated Bibliography

By
COLLEEN
LAHAN MAKOWSKI

The Scarecrow Press, Inc.
Metuchen, N.J., & London
1985

Library of Congress Cataloging in Publication Data

Makowski, Colleen Lahan, 1948–
    Quilting, 1915-1983.

    Includes index.
    1. Quilting--Bibliography. I. Title.
Z6153.Q54M34 1985   016.74646   85-2497
[TT835]
ISBN 0-8108-1813-2

CONTENTS

ACKNOWLEDGMENTS

I wish to thank the many people who have contributed to this book: Catherine Mager and Ruth Bennett who typed the manuscript, Patricia Parker for her suggestions, the fine librarians in Buffalo.

This bibliography would not have been possible without the excellent library facilities in Western New York: the Buffalo and Erie County Public Library, the E. H. Butler Library at Buffalo State College, the library of the Albright Knox Art Gallery, and the Lockwood Library at SUNY, Buffalo.

Also, many thanks to the museum directors in the United States, Canada, and the United Kingdom for assisting me in this research.

I also want to thank my parents, Maurice and Mary Lahan, my husband, Joe, and Debbie and Brad Moncton for watching Matthew while I worked on this project.

Pieced-Work Bedcover. Log Cabin pattern in Barn Raising arrangement; 5,500 pieces; silk. Made in Lewisburg, Pa., late nineteenth
century. Smithsonian Institution Photo No. 76-2663.

I. BOOKS

1. Alfers, Betty. Quilting: Over 50 Attractive Designs for You to Piece, Appliqué, Embroider, and Stuff. New York: Bobbs-Merrill, 1978, 196pp.
   Black-and-white and color illustrations. Discusses techniques for making templates, selecting and cutting fabric, piecing, appliquéing, stuffing, quilting and finishing the quilt. Chapter on tools, designs for clothing and accessories (aprons, skirts, shirts, bags). Designs for children (bibs, stuffed toys, sleeping bags, circus quilt, Mother Goose quilt). Designs for the home (table cover, wall hanging, pillows, pincushions and Christmas decorations, tea cozy, toaster cover and other kitchen items). Designs for classic quilts: Victoria, Strawberry, Rob Peter to Pay Paul, Double Irish Cross and Whig Rose. Full-size patterns, notes finished size of quilt, blocks, materials needed, and directions.

2. Anders, Nedda C. Appliqué Old and New, Including Patchwork and Embroidery. New York: Dover, 1976, 128pp.
   Includes index, nine-item bibliography. Frontispiece is mid-nineteenth century English appliquéd coverlet. Black-and-white illustrations and photos. Chapters on materials needed and design techniques, methods, types of appliqué (including bead, braid, ribbon and cord), stitches employed in its use, method for inlay work and ecclesiastical appliqué. Directions for flower bouquet wall hanging with materials needed and illustrated steps. Use of appliqué in patchwork quilts and potholders and the use of the sewing machine. Directions for Presidents Wreath; chapters on teaching appliqué to children and contemporary appliqué. Twenty-one illustrated embroidery stitches. Many photos of items in the Victoria and Albert Museum.

3. Anthony, Ilid. Quilting and Patchwork in Wales. St. Fagan's, Cardiff, Wales: Welsh Folk Museum, 1972, 15pp.
   Discusses the history of quilting and patchwork in bedcovers and clothing. Also published in Amgueddfa, Bulletin of the National Museum of Wales.

4. Auld, Rhoda L. Molas. New York: Van Nostrand Reinhold, 1977, 112pp.
   Includes bibliography and index, black-and-white and color photos. Discussion of Cuna women's mode of dressing, appliqué and use of many 3-, 4- and 6-color mola reverse appliqués, collecting and using molas in home decoration, and making paper cutouts.

1

5. Avery, Virginia. Big Book of Appliqué: For Quilts and Ban-
    ners, Clothes, Hangings, Gifts and More. New York: Charles
    Scribner's Sons, 1978, 160pp.
         Photos and illustrations. Directions for projects from be-
    ginning to end.

6. Bacon, Lenice Ingram. American Patchwork Quilts. New York:
    William Morrow and Co., 1973, 190pp.
         Forty-eight pages of color, and black-and-white photos of
    quilts in museums and private collections. Includes bibliography
    and an index. History of patchwork and appliqué, with chapters on
    buying, collecting, caring for and repairing old quilts. Covers
    European, American, Hawaiian, Victorian and Renaissance quilts.
    Includes stories and photos of quilts, accompanied by their history,
    description and location. Examples: Log Cabin, Baby Blocks
    and Pineapple (1791).

7. Bannister, Barbara and Ford, Edna P., eds. State Capitals
    Quilt Blocks: Fifty Patchwork Patterns from 'Hearth and Home'
    Magazine. New York: Dover, 1977, 71pp.
         These patterns were chosen by the editors from a Hearth
    and Home contest on the basis of originality. The blocks for Alaska
    and Hawaii are from another Hearth and Home contest. Full-size
    patterns for fifty state capitals with short histories of each capital
    city. Finished quilt size, number of blocks, size of border and
    fabric requirements are noted. Includes commentary by the original
    contributor. Sixteen color blocks are shown on the front and back
    covers.

8. _____ and _____, eds. The United States Patchwork Pat-
    tern Book: Fifty Quilt Blocks for Fifty States from 'Hearth and
    Home' Magazine. New York: Dover, 1976, 76pp.
         Collection of block patterns issued for the bicentennial. Not
    an instructional book. Included are: black-and-white illustrations
    of each block, full-size patterns, size of finished quilt, fabric re-
    quirements and number of blocks needed. Short statement on each
    block given by the person who submitted it to the magazine. Six-
    teen color blocks are shown on the front and back covers. These
    patterns were contributed by readers as part of the magazine's
    State Block Pattern series from 1907 to 1912.

9. Barnes, Christine. Quilting--Patchwork, Appliqué, 2nd ed.
    Menlo Park, Calif.: Lane Publishing Co., 1982, 88pp.
         Revised edition of Quilting and Patchwork, (1973). Includes
    index and color photos. Sections on patchwork and quilting tech-
    niques and directions with color illustrations. How to estimate yard-
    age, design, color and scale. Special attention to curved seams,
    hexagons, Long Cabin and string quilts. Short discussion of quilt
    care, appliqué, curves, corners, points and variations of appliqué
    (e.g., multilayer, padded, and reverse. Also discusses piecing,
    using the sewing machine, and finishing). Part 2 offers the follow-
    ing projects with fabric requirements and directions: Pillows, table-
    cloth, placemats, crib quilt, child's vest, jacket, purse and quilts.

Part 3 consists of seventeen pages of color photos of quilts: Amish, various pieced quilts, Log Cabins, appliqué, album quilts and modern quilts and their uses in the home.   Also notes where the quilts are housed.

10.   Better Homes & Gardens.   Appliqué.   Des Moines, Iowa: Meredith Corp. , 1978, 96pp.
        Contains an index of designers' names, four pages of instructions, a color photo of each finished item (e. g. , pillows, banner, baby quilt, bed quilt, wall panel and reverse appliqué wall hanging).   Patterns are shown reduced on graph paper.   Also gives fabric requirements and includes a chapter on creative appliqué.

11.   _____.   Patchwork and Quilting.   Des Moines, Iowa: Meredith Corp. , 1977, 96pp.
        Forty color photos of finished projects with black-and-white illustrations.   Instructions for small items such as placemats, tablecloths, curtains and quilts.   Some patterns shown: Attic Window, Joseph's Coat, Kings Cross, Dresden Plate and Wildflowers.   Shows how to transfer children's crayon drawings onto cloth to make a quilt. No full-size patterns.

12.   Beyer, Alice.   Quilting.   Chicago: South Park Commissioners, 1934, 76pp.
        Prepared in the Recreation Department, Leisure Hobbies Series.   Published just after the Chicago World's Fair of 1933.   This has been reprinted by the East Bay Heritage Quilters, Box 6223, Albany, Calif. 94706, 1978.   Black-and-white photo of Eleanor Roosevelt receiving the first-prize quilt in A Century of Progress exhibition.   Illustrations of the block that won first prize at the fair and a sketch of the completed quilt.   Gives the steps in quiltmaking, materials needed and stitches used.   Illustrates some traditional block patterns.   Suggestions for borders, designing original patterns and a method for enlarging patterns.   Two-page bibliography.

13.   Beyer, Jinny.   The Art and Technique of Creating Medallion Quilts.   McLean, Va.:   EPM Publications, 1982, 169pp.
        Discusses the history of medallion quilts.   Gives construction directions, accompanied by photos and illustrations of modern and antique medallion quilts.   Includes bibliography and index.

14.   _____.   Patchwork Patterns.   McLean, Va.: EPM Publications, 1979, 200pp.
        Includes index of pattern names.   Primarily black-and-white photos and illustrations, some color photos.   Instructional book for analyzing geometric patterns and drafting templates using various methods, tools and techniques such as a compass, draftsman's triangle and paper folding.   Gives numerous illustrations of various patchwork patterns.   Relates the similarity of the patterns in each category to facilitate user analysis.   Also includes curved patchwork, stars, hexagons and kaleidoscope.

15.   _____.   A Quilter's Album of Blocks and Borders.   McLean, Va.:   EPM Publications, 1980, 198pp.

Over 700 designs with directions for pattern drafting. Gives
the name of the design and its reference source. Black-and-white
photos and drawings and a bibliography. Discusses how to use
printed fabric in quilts, and sources for quilt patterns. Categorizes
various geometric designs. Includes footnotes and an index.

16.   Bishop, Robert.   The Knopf Collector's Guide to American An-
       tiques: Quilts, Coverlets, Rugs and Samplers.   New York: Ran-
       dom House, 1982, 480pp.
            Two-hundred color photos of quilts.   Includes bibliography,
glossary, and index.   Examples of nineteenth- and twentieth-century
quilts with price range.

17.   _____ and Coblentz, P.   New Discoveries in American Quilts.
       New York: E. P. Dutton, 1975, 127pp.
            Authors consider it a supplement to the book America's
Quilts and Coverlets (1972).   Sixteen categories of quilts; bed rugs,
linsey-woolsey, whole cloth, pieced, Amish, Log Cabin, appliqué,
Hawaiian, candlewick, stencil, stuffed work and children's quilts,
chapter on Susan McCord, crazy quilts and patriotic quilts.   Includes
240 photos, 160 in color, and a bibliography.   Quilts described date
from the mid-seventeenth century to the present.

18.   _____ and Safanda, Elizabeth.   A Gallery of Amish Quilts--
       Design Diversity from a Plain People.   New York: E. P. Dut-
       ton, 1976, 96pp.
            Discusses the spiritual and cultural roots of Amish society;
woman's position in that society and the origins of the Amish quilt.
Covers piecing the quilt, bees, dyes and fabric used; origin of pattern and quilt designs, both pieced and quilt and evolution of the
quilt.   Photos of medallion, diamond square, Lone Star, bars, Sunshine & Shadow, crazy, nine-patch, Log Cabins, whole cloth and
Baskets, all from Pennsylvania.   From the Midwest: Tree of Life,
Double Nine-Patch, Hexagons, Baskets, Barn Raising, Star and crib
quilts.   Accompanied by bibliography and footnotes.

19.   Bogan, Constance.   A Beginner's Book of Patchwork, Applique
       and Quilting.   New York: Dodd, Mead & Co., 1974, 159pp.
            Basic instructions, index, black-and-white photos and illus-
trations with descriptions.   Full-size patterns include Peony and Fan.
Chapter on appliqué patterns includes Trees, Rose and Sunbonnet
Children.   Also gives quilting patterns and embroidery stitches.   Examples of items to make: potholder, wall hanging and pillow with
patterns.   Gives fabric requirements and directions.   Several photos
from the Metropolitan Museum of Art collection.   Also gives directions for a Log Cabin quilt.

20.   Bond, Dorothy.   Crazy Quilt Stitches.   Cottage Grove, Ore.:
       By the Author, 1981, 112pp.
            Twenty-two categories of stitches from old American quilts.
Illustrates over 1,000 plain, decorative and combination stitches, including some previously published in her book Embroidery Stitches
(1977).

21. _____. Embroidery Stitches from Old American Quilts.
Cottage Grove, Ore.: By the Author, 1977, 40pp., out of print.
Illustrates 400 stitches, simple and ornate, used on old
quilts. Also illustrates thread.

22. Bonesteel, Georgia. Lap Quilting with Georgia Bonesteel. Birmingham, Ala.: Oxmoor House, 1982, 122pp.
Book includes an index of designs and patterns in addition
to a general index. Introduction to terminology, fabric and design.
Full-size patterns, directions for piecing the block, and quilting it
and assembling the quilt in the lap-quilting method. Black-and-white
illustrations. Projects: tote bags, table runner, aprons, vests and
pillows. Notes materials needed, method and fabric requirements.

23. Brackman, Barbara. An Encyclopedia of Pieced Quilt Patterns.
Lawrence, Kan.: By the Author, 1979-1983, 8 vols., 604pp.
A loose-leaf book showing quilt block patterns that are
categorized as: v.1: All-over patterns; v.2: Realistic; v.3: Four-
Patches; v.4: Nine-Patches; v.5: Square in a Square; v.6: Nine X.;
v.7: Wheels and Fans; v.8: Stars, and Miscellaneous. Includes
an index with pattern name and source. Each volume includes ten
full-size patterns for blocks shown.

24. Bray, Karen. Machine Appliqué. Walnut Creek, Calif.: By
the Author, 1978, 48pp.   .
Presently out of print, but the author hopes to revise it
in the near future. Gives instructions for smaller items. Illustrated with drawings and photographs.

25. Breckenridge, Muriel. Lap Quilting. New York: Sterling Publishing Co., 1981, 96pp.
Method for sewing quilts in a small amount of space. Includes index, black-and-white illustrations and eight pages of color
photos. Chapters on materials needed, marking fabric, appliqué,
quilting on a lap frame and estimating yardage. Projects: pillows,
Log Cabin quilt, bag, placemats, table runners, small items and
Christmas projects. Discusses method for using a tapestry frame,
larger hoop and/or a lap board for smaller pieces.

26. Brondolo, Barbara. Small Patchwork Projects, with Step-by-
Step Instructions and Full-Size Templates. New York: Dover,
1981, 76pp.
Items to make: Hostess apron, wall hangings, evening
bag, bibs, tote bag, placemats, floor pillow and more. Black-and-
white illustrations, color cover. Two pages of general directions,
forty-eight pages of templates, twenty-eight pages of text.

27. Brown, Elsa. Creative Quilting. New York: Watson-Guptill,
1975, 144pp.
Includes an index, bibliography, and a list of where to
purchase supplies. Black-and-white photos and illustrations. Color
frontispiece. Shows trapunto and clothing as well as printed, painted

and dyed fabrics. Discussion of line, form, texture, color, rhythm
and enlarging a design. Emphasis is on modern work.

28.   Carter, Hazel. Bee Quilting Resource Booklet. Washington,
      D. C.: Smithsonian Institution Traveling Exhibition Service,
      1979, 8pp.
            Lists quilting organizations, mail-order businesses, classes,
      books and magazines.

29.   Cerny, Donna and McKenny, Lucinda. Appliquétions: A Source
      Book of Designs and Projects. Rochester, N. H.: By the author,
      1980, 35pp.
            Full-size patterns and directions for smaller items. In-
      cludes tea cozy, glasses case, sewing box, tote and wall hangings.

30.   Chapman, Suzanne. Early American Design Motifs. 2nd. ed.
      New York: Dover, 1974, 138pp.
            Black-and-white illustrations of floral designs, landscapes,
      birds and animals, borders and miscellaneous. Five color photos
      of quilts. Design examples from the Metropolitan Museum of Art;
      Museum of Fine Arts, Boston; Philadelphia Museum of Art, the
      Winterthur Museum and others. Eleven-item bibliography.

31.   Chase, Judith. Afro-American Art and Craft. New York: Van
      Nostrand Reinhold Co., 1971, 142pp.
            Traces appliqué back to Egypt, Europe and Dahomey. Dis-
      cusses quilting, fabric and technique. Four black-and-white photos.
      Treatment of quilting pp. 88-90.

32.   Chase, Pattie and Dolbier, Mimi. The Contemporary Quilt:
      New American Quilts and Fabric Art. Foreword by Radka Don-
      nell. New York: E. P. Dutton, 1978, 80pp.
            Contains 141 photos of fabric art, biographical information
      on the artists and an index. Statements by the artists on their work.
      Divides examples into abstract, graphic, dreamlike and three-
      dimensional.

33.   Chatterton, Pauline. Patchwork and Appliqué. New York: The
      Dial Press, 1977, 214pp.
            Instructional. Discusses fabric, tools, templates, and
      planning a project for both patchwork and appliqué. Includes smaller
      items such as cushions and wall hanging. Goes into some of the
      fold themes for appliqué and shows the work of contemporary artists.
      Black-and-white photos and illustrations. Color photos of original
      designs. Instructions with diagrams for patchwork crochet, crocheted
      appliqué, patchwork knitting, bargello, patchwork and Gobelin.

34.   Christensen, Jo Ippolito. Trapunto--Decorative Quilting. New
      York: Sterling Publishing Co., 1972, 48pp.
            Instructional, with color and black-and-white photos. Black-
      and white-illustrations. Directions for making pillows, pictures,
      aprons, potholders, bibs and baby clothes. Adult items of clothing
      including slippers, a long skirt and a purse.

35. _____ and Shapiro, Sonie. Appliqué and Reverse Appliqué. New York: Sterling Publishing Co., 1974, 48pp.
Index, black-and-white and color illustrations. Examples of appliqué using various media (glue, contact paper); hand and machine-stitched appliqué and molas.

36. Clarke, Mary W. Kentucky Quilts and Their Makers. Lexington: University of Kentucky Press, 1976, 120pp.
Includes material from the Western Kentucky University Folklore and Folklife Collection, including interviews and photographs illustrating the social history of quiltmakers. Contains an index to quiltmaker's names and an index to pattern names. Fifteen-item bibliography. Color and black-and-white photos. Describes a modern quilting bee. Discusses family quilters and persons who quilt alone. Gives examples of Lone Star (1975), an album quilt, Improved Nine-Patch (1970), Ship Yard (1970), Star of Chamblie (late-nineteenth century), Poplar Leaf (1974) and Snake Trail (pre-World War II). Discusses quiltmakers and their work. Chapter on patterns found in Kentucky. Uses the artists' terminology.

37. Colby, Averil. Patchwork. Newton Center, Mass.: Charles T. Branford, 1958, 201pp.
Discusses the early history, materials, tools, geometrical patterns, geometrical designs and color for block quilts, strip quilts, all-over quilts and framed quilts. Also shows Log Cabin, crazy, applied work, inlay, onlay, templates, lining and finishing, all in the English method from the eighteenth through the twentieth centuries. Examples of: diamond based on a hexagon, Box pattern, Double Star, Brick pattern and rectangles set at angle for border. Also includes Isle of Wight coverlet and Durham Flower Basket quilt.

38. _____. Patchwork Quilts. New York: Charles Scribner's Sons, 1965, 94pp.
Technical discussion of English patchwork, with illustrations of both English and American work. Photos of the quilt at Levan's Hall, an eighteenth-century marriage coverlet, a late-eighteenth-century Star of Bethlehem (color), a Broderie Perse spread from the eighteenth century and a Wellington commemorative quilt, c.1813 (color). Also illustrates applied-work coverlets and a nineteenth-century silk quilt. Examples of hexagon work and a Barn Raising quilt from the nineteenth century. Includes instructions and diagrams.

39. _____. Quilting. New York: Charles Scribner's Sons, 1971, 212pp.
Discusses quilting from the earliest time to the present. Directions for wadded, flat, corded and stuffed quilting and gathered patchwork. Considered a reference work. Black-and-white photos of clothing and bedcovers.

40. Conroy, Mary. 300 Years of Canada's Quilts. Toronto: Griffin House, 1976, 133pp.
Relates the history of quiltmaking in Canada from its introduction in New France to its revival from 1950 through the 1970's.

Lists where to see quilts in Canada. Categorizes quilting by date
from the early nineteenth century, mid-century, 1867 through 1900,
1900 through 1914, World War I, 1918 through 1928, the Depression,
World War II through the postwar period and 1950 through the 1970's.
Color and black-and-white photos, line drawings and a bibliography.
Fifteen patterns given for some of the illustrated quilts: Swallow in
the Path, LeMoyne Star, Double Pyramids and Wreath of Roses.
Notes size of finished quilt, fabric requirements, border size and
how to set the blocks. Color cover.

41.   Cooper, Patricia and Buferd, Norma G. The Quilters: Women
      and Domestic Art. New York: Doubleday, 1977, 157pp.
            Text taken from tapes and notes of conversations between
quilters and the authors in Texas and New Mexico. Photos of the
women quilting and photos of the geography of the region. Discusses
the influence of the environment on their work. Color photos of
quilts, primarily pieced, with black-and-white photos of the women.

42.   Corwin, Judith. Easy to Make Appliqué Quilts for Children.
      New York: Dover, 1982, 48pp.
            Twelve full-size patterns with instructions for appliqué
quilts such as owl and elephant. Also shows smaller items.

43.   Costabel-Deutsch, Eva. Design and Make Your Own Floral
      Appliqué: With Full-Size Templates and Step-by-Step Instructions.
      New York: Dover, 1976, 40pp.
            Seven appliqué designs. Instructions on cutting the shapes,
appliquéing (two methods), using the sewing machine and using deli-
cate fabrics. Illustrates embroidery stitches, and gives directions
for washing embroidery. Twenty-four pages of templates, including
cover designs and sixteen pages of instructions.

44.   Cox, Patricia. Every Stitch Counts. Minneapolis: By the Au-
      thor, 1982, 100pp.
            One hundred full-size original or traditional patterns for
12-, 13-, and 14-inch squares. Color cover.

45.   _____. The Log Cabin Workbook. Minneapolis: By the Au-
      thor, 1980, 64pp.
            One hundred twenty original Log Cabin quilt layouts, with
directions, diagrams and yardage charts. Color covers.

46.   Danneman, Barbara. Step-by-Step Quiltmaking. New York:
      Golden Press, 1975, 80pp.
            Nine-item bibliography. Lists suppliers in the United States.
Black-and-white and color photos of finished quilts. Examples of
pieced and appliquéd tops. Gives basic quiltmaking directions. Projects such as Around the World Quilt, Log Cabin Pocketbook, pre-
Stuffed Triangles Quilt, wall hanging, cathedral window quilt and
trapunto work.

47.   Davis, Marlene. A Nova Scotia Work Basket. Halifax, Nova
      Scotia: Nova Scotia Museum, 1976, pp. 44-69.
            Discussion of Nova Scotian quilts.

48. Davis, Rita. Simple Yet Stunning Quilts. Portland, Ore.:
    R. C. Publications, 1982, 66pp.
         Instructions for machine quilts with full-size pattern tem-
    plates. Includes planning and yardage charts for various size quilts.
    Over fifty black-and-white photos showing steps of constructions.
    Color photos of finished quilts. Written for the beginner.

49. Dean, Beryl. Creative Appliqué. New York: Watson-Guptill,
    1970, 104pp.
         Emphasis on contemporary work with many examples of
    finished designs. Some antique examples from the Victoria and Al-
    bert Museum and the Smithsonian. Chapters on machine embroidery
    and stitching, appliqué for church and theatre, finishing and mount-
    ing the work. Contains index, bibliography, color cover, four pages
    of color photos and numerous black-and-white photos and illustrations.

50. Donahue, Nancy. Butterflies. Industry, Calif.: By the Au-
    thor, 1982, 128pp.
         Over eighty butterfly patterns: appliquéd, pieced and
    quilted. Instructions for their use on small items. Fifty projects
    including quilts, clocks, wall hangings, pillows and mobiles. Color
    photos of each of the finished projects.

51. _____. Little Patchwork Things. Industry, Calif.: By the
    Author, 1981, 104pp.
         Thirty-nine miniature three-inch quilt patterns. Discusses
    technique. Twenty-one projects for clothing trims, Christmas orna-
    ments and smaller items for the home. Thirty-four color plates
    showing all completed miniature projects.

52. _____. The Quilt As You Go Guide. Industry, Calif.: By
    the Author, 1980, 52pp.
         Directions for constructing quilts by the quilt-as-you-go
    method. Two hundred twenty-seven diagrams, twenty-one color plates
    of finished projects. Section on making smaller items.

53. _____. Shadow Trapunto. Industry, Calif.: By the Author,
    1983, 72pp.
         Color cover. Directions for clothing, quilts, pillows, orna-
    ments and smaller items. Over ninety patterns.

54. Devlin, Nancy. Make It in Minutes with Quick Prequilted 6"
    Squares. Severna Park, Md.: By the Author, 1979, 15pp.
         Instructions for pillows, placemats, quilts and smaller
    items made on the sewing machine. Drawings and color photos il-
    lustrating the technique.

55. Dubois, Jean. The Colonial History Quilt. Evans, Colo.: By
    the Author, 1978, 56pp.
         Patterns for twenty-four blocks designed by Ruby McKim.
    Black-and-white photos. Instructions. Blocks are done in embroi-
    dery.

56. _____. A Galaxy of Stars: America's Favorite Quilts.
    Evans, Colo.: By the Author, 1976, 137pp.
        Pattern book with thirty-three black-and-white quilt photos
and numerous black-and-white illustrations, and directions.   Twenty-
five star patterns, with history.   Includes index and bibliography.
Stars categorized as Ohio, Sawtooth, World Without End and LeMoyne.
Also has chapters on borders.

57. _____. The Wool Quilt: Patterns and Possibilities.   Evans,
    Colo.: By the Author, 1978, 179pp.
        Seventeen patterns such as Yankee Puzzle, Windmill Cross
and Evening Star.   Ninety-six black-and-white photos, diagrams of
Amish quilts and a chapter on appliqué.

58. Dudley, Taimi. Strip Patchwork: Quick and Easy Patchwork
    Using the Seminole Technique. New York: Van Nostrand Rein-
    hold, 1980, 128pp.
        Contains index, metric conversion chart, bibliography,
four pages with color photos of Seminole quilts, wall hangings and
clothing.   Primarily black-and-white illustrations and photos.   Glossary (12 items).   Shows "typical" Seminole patterns with instructions.
Ideas on color, use of light and dark and fabric requirements.   Examples shown: Medallion, Lone Star, Nine-Patch, Log Cabin and
Tulip pattern.   Discusses woolen fabric, clothing, boutique items
and a Christmas banner.   Includes how to adapt the technique to machine sewing.

59. Dunton, William R. Old Quilts. Catonsville, Md.: By the Au-
    thor, 1946, 278pp.
        Color frontispiece, black-and-white plates.   Discusses al-
bum quilts, applied chintz quilts, Tree of Life, framed medallions
and plain quilts, a Masonic quilt, Feathered Star (1844) and album
quilts from 1845, 1846, 1850 and 1847, each accompanied by detailed
description.   Discusses quilting bees and the history of quiltmaking.
One hundred and twenty-five black-and-white plates of quilts.

60. Echols, Margit. The Quilters Coloring Book. New York:
    Thomas Y. Crowell Co., 1979, 223pp.
        Twenty full-size patterns such as Nine-Patch, Jack-in-the-
Box, Fence Rail and Shoo Fly.   Chapters on fabric, stitchery techniques, borders, enlarging a quilt and care of quilts.   Black-and-
white illustrations, four pages of quilts in color, noting name of
quilt, date and fabric.   Four pages for experimenting with color for
a full-size quilt (Road to California) or one of the examples.   Directions for piecing with illustration of the block.   Emphasis on color
experimentation.

61. Elwood, Judy; Tennery, Joyce and Richardson, Alice. Tennes-
    see Quilting Designs Plus Patterns. Oak Ridge, Tenn.: By the
    Authors, 1982, 54pp.

Now in a second printing.   Old and new patterns relating
to the state of Tennessee, accompanied by the history of the state.

62.   Ericson, Helen M.   Friendly Medley: A Set of 10 Pieced and
      Applique Patterns for Classes and Friendship Quilts, Continuing
      the Danner Tradition.   Emporia, Kan.:   By the Author, 1982,
      29pp.
            Two black-and-white photos: Friendly Medley quilt and
      Blue Windmill.   Twenty small, black-and-white photos of individual
      blocks, pieced and appliquéd: Tobacco Leaf, Mexican Rose, Galway
      Star and Fantasy appliqué.   Full-size patterns for each block with
      directions and some illustrations of the finished block.   Also includes
      quilting pattern for cable chain.

63.   _____, ed.   Mrs. Danner's Quilts, Books 1 & 2 Combined.
      2nd ed.   Emporia, Kan.:   By the Author, 1971, 40pp.
            New edition of books one and two originally published in
      1934 by Scioto Imhoff Danner.   Catalog of quilt patterns.   Fifty-six
      black-and-white photos of portions of whole quilts illustrating both
      pieced and appliquéd patterns, accompanied by brief description of
      the pattern and its price, e.g., Lotus Blossom, Spice Pins and
      Wishing Ring.

64.   _____, ed.   Mrs. Danner's Quilts, Books 3 & 4 Combined,
      3rd ed.   Emporia, Kan.:   By the Author, 1973, 34pp.
            New edition of catalogs published by Scioto Imhoff Danner
      in 1954 and 1958.   Forty-seven black-and-white photos of quilt pat-
      terns with prices.   Includes Hollyhocks, Mrs. Anderson's Quilt, Bas-
      ket Triangles and the poem "Patchwork Magic" by N. M. Bennet.

65.   _____, ed.   Mrs. Danner's Fifth Quilt Book, 3rd ed.   Em-
      poria, Kan.:   By the Author, 1979, 27pp.
            Black-and-white photo of Mrs. Danner's house in El Dor-
      ado, Kansas.   Four small black-and-white photos of quilt patterns
      with description and price, e.g., Mayflower, Fredonia Oak Leaf
      and Buttons and Bows.

66.   _____.   Mrs. Danner's Quilts Presents Book Six: Helen's
      Book of Basic Quiltmaking, 2nd ed.   Emporia, Kan.:   By the
      Author, 1979, 27pp.
            Catalog of forty-three black-and-white photos of block pat-
      terns including Blazing Stars, Lady of the Lake and appliquéd Butter-
      flies, accompanied by description, price and ten lessons on making
      a quilt.

67.   _____.   Mrs. Danner's Quilts Presents Book Seven.   Emporia,
      Kan.:   By the Author, 1975, 23pp.
            Thirty-nine black-and-white photos of block patterns, e.g.,
      Sunbonnet Baby, Straw Hat Boy, Doves, Honey Bee and Christmas
      Plume.   Accompanied by description and price.

68.   Fairfield, Helen. Patchwork. London: Octopus Books, 1980,
       80pp.
               Contains index, list of suppliers in the U. S. A. and Great
Britain. Color photos and illustrations. Includes both English and
American method and terminology for piecing patchwork for each
project. Full photos of English hexagon quilt from the 1830's with
directions; mid-nineteenth-century Irish pieced and appliquéd quilt.
Directions for tea cozy, small bag, pillows, alphabet quilt, crib
quilt, Log Cabin quilt and wall hangings.

69.   Fanning, Tony and Fanning, Robbie. The Complete Book of
       Machine Quilting. Radnor, Pa.: Chilton Book Co., 1980, 334pp.
               Extensive list of resources, supplies and bibliography.
How to make adjustments for your machine, dos and don'ts, how to
construct the quilt top, using a presser foot, "free" machine quilting and the quilt-as-you-go method. Quick gifts to make, and directions for constructing designs. Poses problems and offers an-
swers. Glossary; how to estimate yardage requirements.

70.   Field, Clarie C. Quilts: Tie It You'll Like It: A Tied Quilt
       Guide. Farmington, Utah: By the Author, 1981, 42pp.
               Now in its third printing with color photos and a section
on "No Quilt" quilts.

71.   Field, June. Creative Patchwork. London: Pitman Publishing,
       1974, 96pp.
               Contains index, list of suppliers in the United States and
Great Britain; twenty-item bibliography. Eight pages of color photos;
black-and-white photos found on every page. Examples from the
Victoria and Albert Museum, Welsh Folk Museum, Newark Museum,
American Museum in Britain and private collections. Chapters on
history, method, various shapes and the background of various quilts.
Discusses crazy quilts and appliqué, pictorial quilts, clothing, home
decorating and toys. Examples of the many uses of patchwork and
appliqué. More an idea book than instructional.

72.   Finley, Ruth. Old Patchwork Quilts and the Women Who Made
       Them. Philadelphia: J. B. Lippincott, 1929; reprint ed., New-
       ton Centre, Mass.: Charles T. Branford Co., 1980, 202pp.
               Contains index of quilt names, ninety-six black-and-white
photos of quilts with owners' names. One hundred diagrams of block
patterns. Author believes that patchwork quilts provide a record of
our past in their symbolism and in the fact that they were a cottage
industry for two centuries. Notes the year 1880 as the end of an
era. Chapters on the quilting bee, making a quilt, quilt names,
appliqué, borders, and the decline of the craft due to lack of new
patterns.

73.   Fisher, Katherine and Kay, Elizabeth. Quilting in Squares.
       New York: Charles Scribner's Sons, 1978, 127pp.
               Contains bibliography. Illustrated with sixteen pages of
color photos, full-size patterns and a glossary. Examples of patterns: Wreath of Roses, Hens and Chickens appliqué, School House

appliqué, Friendship Wheel, Sunbonnet Sue and Overall Sam. Includes fabric charts.

74. FitzRandolph, Mavis. <u>Traditional Quilting: Its Story and Its</u>
     <u>Practice</u>. London: Batsford, 1954, 168pp.
         Contains index, comparative tables of quilters' earnings in
Northern England and Southern Wales from 1890 through the 1950's.
Chapter on "References to Quilting from the Fifteenth to the Eighteenth Century" and on "Old Joe the Northumberland Quilter, 1745-
1825." Fifty-five photographs. Author states the objective of the
book "is to put on record much of the traditional lore about quilting."
Uses survey of rural industries from 1920 through 1923 in England
and Wales. Historical treatment of the subject. Chapters on the
quilters, how quilts are made, the materials, patterns and the future
of traditional quilting.

75. Fournier, Frances. <u>Quilt It and Wear It</u>. Vancouver, B. C.:
     By the Author, 1981, 66pp.
         Instructional book with illustrations and a bibliography.
Covers the use of patterns and how to make patchwork items of
clothing.

76. Frager, Dorothy. <u>The Quilting Primer</u>. Radnor, Pa.: The
     Chilton Book Co., 1974, 133pp.
         Lists necessary supplies. Discusses brands, and where
to purchase materials; forty-five-word glossary. Instructions on
choosing color and fabric, how to design patterns and an entire
quilt, how to execute patchwork, appliqué and borders. How to
make small items and crib quilts. Examples of easy quilts, and
heirloom quilts. Black-and-white illustrations; black-and-white and
color photos.

77. _____. <u>The Quilting Primer</u>, 2nd. ed. Radnor, Pa.: The
     Chilton Book Co., 1979, 227pp.
         Covers advanced techniques. Color cover, index, eight
pages of color photos, numerous black-and-white photos and illustrations. Chapters on beginning the project, marking the fabric,
quilting and making small items (e.g., placemats, tablecloth, pillow,
apron, potholder, skirts). Chapters on crib quilts and blanket quilting. Photo of Three Bears quilt. Directions for Birds of a Feather
and Bunnies in a Field of Patches. Directions for five easy quilts:
Tulip, Old-Fashioned Patches, Windmills, Rail Fence and Combination. Sections on traditional patterns. Sections on sampler and
pictorial quilts, with short statement on the Ulster County Bicentennial Quilt, Delaware and Hudson Canal Sesquicentennial Quilt, Onondaga County Bicentennial Quilt, Post Mills Vermont Quilt and
Freedom Rider Quilt. Chapter on making a quilt block by block,
using scraps and making crazy quilts. Chapter containing full-size
patterns: rectangles, triangles, circles, diamonds, Mohawk Trail
appliqué, Dresden Plate, Flowers, Butterfly, Leaves, Eagle, School
House, Barrister's Block, Pine Trees and Sunbonnet Sue.

78. _____. Start Off in Boutique Quilting. Radnor, Pa.: Chilton Book Co., 1974, 26pp.
   Chapters on placemats, tablecloths, pillows, clothing, crib quilts and potholders. Color cover, black-and-white illustrations and photos. Directions for hand and machine quilting. Illustrations of various patterns: Variable Star, Monkey Wrench and Geese to the Moon.

79. Gammell, Alice I. Polly Prindle's Book of American Patchwork Quilts. rev. by Patricia Newkirk. New York: Grosset and Dunlap, 1976, 238pp.
   Fifty full-size patterns for patchwork and appliqué. Notes yardage requirements and finished quilt size. Some border patterns given. Gives brief history of the craft and explains eight steps for making a quilt. Discusses color, fabric, and mitering a corner. Black-and-white photos illustrating steps in the procedure.

80. Gillies, Jean. Patterns for Appliqué and Pieced Work, and Ways to Use Them. Philadelphia, Pa.: Farm Journal, Inc., 1982, 130pp.
   Contains index, color photos, black-and-white illustrations, seventy-five full-size patterns. Instructions for making fifty items including appliqués for clothes, quilts and bags. Directions and illustrations for appliqué by hand and machine; quilting and embroidery stitches. Directions and illustrations for pillows, tote bag, placemats, potholders, crib quilts, bibs, shoulder bag and stuffed ornaments (star, bird, heart, butterfly and clowns). Color photos of finished projects. Gives fabric requirements and directions.

81. Gobes, Sara; Robbins, J.; Lawler, M. and Meyer, S. Not Just Another Quilt. New York: Van Nostrand Reinhold, 1982, 160pp.
   Contains index, metric conversion chart, and a forty-one item glossary. Eight pages of color photos of finished quilts, black-and-white photos, full-size patterns, cutting chart, color placement diagram of quilt, twenty modern designs with short description. Notes material required, finished size, step-by-step piecing instructions and directions for quilting and finishing, with illustrations. Gives the basics of quilting, displaying the quilt, mounting and stretching it on a frame. Includes statements by the authors.

82. Gonin, Eileen and Newton, Jill. Quiltmaking for Your Home. London: Octopus Books, 1974, 128pp.
   Thirty-two color photos of finished items such as Double Wedding Ring, Birds of Paradise, Sunbonnet Sue quilts, pinafore dress, reversible jacket, bib and a batik picture. Instructions accompanied by color illustrations and full-size patterns for trapunto, quilting, patchwork and appliqué. Photos of quilts from the American Museum in Britain such as mosaic, dated from the 1860's; Log Cabin; Star of Bethlehem, dated late-nineteenth century; Double Wedding Ring, dated 1930. Basic general instructions, yardage requirements, and directions for stuffed work, contour and a simple Hawaiian quilt.

Examples of some of the items to make: denim quilt, marriage
quilt, cushions and beach bag.   Frontispiece shows the Hudson River
quilt.

83.   Gonsalves, Alyson, ed.   Quilting and Patchwork.   Menlo Park,
      Calif.:   Lane Books, 1973, 80pp.
            Twenty-four item glossary, both color, and black-and-
white photos.   Illustrations of construction techniques.   Discusses
use of the sewing machine, items such as placemats, vests, ties,
tote bag and a Hawaiian quilt.   Also discusses quiltmaking tools,
color, design, pattern drafting, borders, hexagons, appliqué, tying
and stuffed work.

84.   Grafton, Carol B.   Early American Patchwork Patterns.   New
      York: Dover, 1980, 65pp.
            Twelve full-size block patterns such as School House, Log
Cabin and Flower Basket.

85.   _____.   Geometric Patchwork Patterns: Full Size Cut-Outs
      and Instructions for Twelve Quilts.   New York: Dover, 1975,
      63pp.
            Five pages of introductory material.   Twelve patterns, ac-
companied by a sketch of the whole quilt.   Gives directions, size,
fabric requirements, number of pieces to be cut and color illustrations of the finished block.   E.g., Double Z, Stone Mason's Puzzle,
Brunswick Star, Box quilt, Georgetown Circle and Solomon's Temple.

86.   _____.   Traditional Patchwork Patterns.   New York: Dover,
      1974, 57pp.
            Full-size templates and instructions for twelve quilts.   Gives
sketch of the whole quilt, size, materials needed, number of pieces
to be cut and color illustrations of each block.   E.g., Starlight,
Double Irish Chain, Barrister's Block, Pineapple and Tree of Paradise.

87.   Grandmother Clark's Old Fashioned Quilt Designs.   St. Louis,
      Mo.:   W. L. M. Clark Inc., 1931, reprint ed., Alanson, Mich.:
      Barbara Bannister, 1972, 15pp.
            Thirty-six illustrations of quilt blocks with full-size patterns
including Sunburst, Royal Star, Fancy Butterfly, Diamonds, Water-
mill and Chinese Puzzle.   Cover: Book No. 21.

88.   Grandmother Clark's Patchwork Quilt Designs (Book No. 20).
      St. Louis, Mo.:   W. L. M. Clark Inc., 1931; reprint ed.,
      Alanson, Mich.:   Barbara Bannister, 1973, 15pp.
            Cover pictures a star quilt.   Full-size patterns for thirty
quilt blocks including Double Wedding Ring, Fancy Star, Pot of Flowers, Windmill and Sunflower.   Accompanied by black-and-white illustrations of the completed block.   Page fifteen shows black-and-
white illustrations of nine quilts using the block patterns in the book.

89.   Grandmother's Authentic Early American Patchwork Quilts (Book

(Book No. 23). St. Louis, Mo.: W. L. M. Clark Inc., 1932;
reprint ed., Alanson, Mich.: Barbara Bannister, 1973, 15pp.
    Full-size patterns for thirty-two designs including Victoria's
Crown, Aunt Eliza's Star, Flower Wreath, Drunkard's Trail and
Laurel Wreath. Some illustrations of the finished quilts. Some designs date to the eighteenth century.

90.   Green Sylvia. Patchwork for Beginners. New York: Watson-
       Guptill, 1972, 104pp.
           Primarily black-and-white photos. Chapters on equipment
needed, patterns, fabric and geometric shapes. Discusses design
and color. Examples of cathedral window, toys and small items.
Instructional book.

91.   Gutcheon, Beth. The Perfect Patchwork Primer. New York:
       David McKay Co., Inc., 1973, 267pp.
           Instructional book with illustrations and directions for mak-
ing patterns. Includes index, suppliers and black-and-white illustrations and photos. Instructions on choosing and preparing fabric,
making templates, marking and sewing the quilt and quilting the top.
Instructions for toys, baby quilts and decorative items. No patterns
given.

92.   _____ and Gutcheon, Jeffrey. The Quilt Design Workbook.
       New York: Rawson Associates Publishers Inc., 1976, 176pp.
           Illustrations of Amish quilts and the authors' own work.
Instructions for creating designs.

93.   Gutcheon, Jeffrey. Diamond Patchwork. New York: Gutcheon
       Patchworks, Inc., 1982, 72pp.
           Both color and black-and-white photos. Full-size patterns.
Instructions for turning squares into diamonds.

94.   Haders, Phyllis. Sunshine and Shadow: The Amish and Their
       Quilts. New York: Universe Books, 1976, 71pp.
           History of the Amish people and the role quilting has played
in their lives. Biblical quotations illustrating various examples of
Amish quilts, accompanied by black-and-white detail quilt photo such
as stars and diamonds. Photos annotated with description, size, date,
maker's name and history. Also gives origin, if known, and fabric
used.

95.   _____. The Warner's Collector's Guide to American Quilts.
       New York: Warner Books Inc., 1981, 255pp.
           Identification guide. Quilts classified as pieced, appliqué
and white-work. One hundred color plates. Over 300 black-and-
white photos. Pertinent information on each quilt, including owner's
name and price range.

96.   Hagerman, Betty. A Meeting of the Sunbonnet Children. Bald-
       win City: By the Author, 1979, 80pp.
           Color frontispiece of the author's quilt, A Meeting of the
Sunbonnet Children with notes on source for each block. Textual

discussion of the patterns' origins, including pattern companies, de-
signers, the Sunbonnet Babies Primer, cards and syndicated needlework columns. Block illustrations of the various Sunbonnets. Full-
size patterns for Sunbonnets and Overall Boy (pp. 56-78) noting origin and date. Twenty-five patterns in all. Also lists suppliers and
bibliography.

97. Hake, Elizabeth. English Quilts, Old and New. London: B. T.
     Batsford, Ltd., 1937, 23pp.
          Black-and-white photos. E. g., Devon quilts (1840 and 1750)
and Somerset quilt (1807), with description. Includes index. Photos
of quilted clothing: Cornish (1837); Herefordshire, early nineteenth
century; Wiltshire; corded quilt from Leicestershire and items from
Wales and Durham. Illustration of an old English quilting frame.
Discusses history, designs, technique and current trends and the
future.

98. Halgrimson, Jan. Great Scrap-bag Quilts. Edmonds, Wash.:
     Weaver Finch Publications, 1980, 108pp.
          Over 100 full-size quilt patterns requiring scraps of fabric.
Includes variations of a full-size Dresden Plate pattern for a sampler
quilt, Bachelor's Puzzle, Gardener's Prize and Grecian Star.

99. _____. Patching Things Up. Edmonds, Wash.: Weaver
     Finch Publications, 1983, 102pp.
          Over 165 full-size patterns drawn in several sizes. Four
color pages. E. g., Allison's Choice, Cassiopia Crow's Foot and
Sweet Willy.

100. _____. Scraps Can Be Beautiful. Edmonds, Wash.:
     Weaver Finch Publications, 1979, 106pp.
          Illustrates over 100 full-size patterns and gives fabric
suggestions. E. g., Aunt Jurusha, Broken Wheel and Joseph's Coat.

101. Hall, Carolyn V. Stitched and Stuffed Art: Contemporary
     Designs for Quilts, Toys, Pillows, Soft Sculpture and Wall
     Hangings. New York: Doubleday, 1974, 186pp.
          Primarily black-and-white photos; four pages of color
photos. Chapters on contemporary quilts, pillows, soft sculpture,
toys, and wall hangings. Also discusses experimental and environ-
mental designs using plastic, fibers and symbolism. Photos annotated with title of the item shown, its size, and the artist's name.
Notes awards and exhibitions for the work shown. Not an instructional book.

102. Hall, Carrie A. and Kretsinger, Rose G. The Romance of
     the Patchwork Quilt in America. New York: Bonanza Books,
     1935, 299pp.
          Part One by Carrie Hall gives the origin and history of
quiltmaking, accompanied by photos of block patterns. Discusses
quilt names, the quilting bee, its place in art and historical quilts.
Part Two, also by Carrie Hall, discusses Colonial and contemporary
quilts. Includes poem "My Mother's Quilts" by Carrie O'Neal.

Black-and-white photos of quilts, with short description and owner's name. Part Three, by Rose Kretsinger, discusses the art of quilting and quilting designs. E.g., Cross Patch, Tree of Life, Kite's Tail, Honey Bee and Sunbonnet Baby. Includes poems on quilting by S. W. Middleton, Carlie Sexton, Irene Cohen and Carrie Hall. Includes index.

103. Hassel, Carla. You Can Be a Super Quilter: A Teach Yourself Manual for Beginners. Des Moines: Wallace-Homestead Book Co., 1980, 120pp.
    Instructions on how to piece, appliqué and quilt. Full-size templates, color photographs and yardage tables. Includes index, thirty-four-item glossary, four pages of color photos, many black-and-white illustrations. Introductory chapters on getting started, piecing squares, triangles, borders, hexagons and curves. Directions on constructing a Dresden Plate quilt. Discussion of puff patch and cathedral window quilt. Also includes frame quilting and quilting designs.

104. _____. You Can Be A Super Quilter II. Des Moines, Iowa: Wallace-Homestead Book Co., 1983, 192pp.
    Discusses pattern drafting techniques, color, and fabric requirements. Includes bibliography, index, templates, black-and-white illustrations and color photos.

105. Haywood, Dixie. The Contemporary Crazy Quilt Project Book. Crown Publishers, 1977, 96pp.
    Update on the Victorian crazy quilt. Black-and-white photos and instructive drawings. Color pictures and directions for projects.

106. _____. Crazy Quilting With A Difference. Pensacola, Fla.: Scissortail Publications, 1981, 88pp.
    Twenty-five color plates, over 100 black-and-white photos and forty-eight charts and drawings. Directions for twenty-four projects for gift and decorator items, clothing and five quilts.

107. Heard, Audrey and Pryor, Beverly. Complete Guide to Quilting. Des Moines, Iowa.: Meredith Corp., 1974, 285pp.
    Includes bibliography of twenty-five books and a forty-five-word glossary. Discusses settings, fabric, tools, hoops, frames and using the sewing machine. Shows how to draft the quilting pattern, estimate yardage and how to do original work in patchwork and appliqué. Examples of ten quilts. Also illustrates clothing and small items for the home.

108. Hechtilinger, Adelaide. American Quilts, Quilting and Patchwork. Harrisburg, Pa.: Stackpole Books, 1974, 358pp.
    Contains index, list of suppliers, publishing houses, shops, collections and nationally known quilting groups. Black-and-white and color photos. Full-size pattern for appliqué, pieced work and quilting. E.g., Circuit Riders and Grandmother's designs. Contains reprint of Chapter Three of Aunt Jane of Kentucky.

Thirty-eight-item glossary of pattern names and a chapter on pieced
work. Designs from the Ladies Art Company Catalog and Nimble
Needle Treasures (1973). Instructions for smaller items and a chapter on collecting.

109. Heirloom Quilts to Treasure: Thirty Traditional Patterns for
     Piecing and Appliquéing. Birmingham, Ala.: Oxmoor House,
     1971, 39pp.
         Compiled and edited by the editors of the Progressive
Farmer magazine. Full-size patterns with black-and-white illustrations of the finished blocks and tips on construction. E.g., Roses
of Picardy, Our Village Green, Lily Corners, Sunbonnet Girl. Brief
essays on the history of the American quilt, making a quilt and the
use of color.

110. Heynes, Anne. Quilting and Patchwork. Leicester, Eng.:
     Dryad Handicrafts, n.d., 16pp.
         Five black-and-white plates of child's bonnet, tea cozy,
cushions and a quilt. Black-and-white illustrations of quilting and
patchwork designs; Box pattern, Pavement, Chinese Block and Star.
Discussion of the technique and history of quilting. Seven-item bibliography on needlework.

111. Higgins, Murial. New Designs for Machine Patchwork. New
     York: Charles Scribner's Sons, 1980, 144pp.
         Contains index, list of suppliers in the United States and
England. Sixteen item bibliography. Color cover, color photos and
black-and-white photos and illustrations. The examples shown originated from Eastern and Middle Eastern designs. Explores the difference between hand and machine work. Notes materials and supplies needed, pattern drafting, cutting and sewing, special techniques
and problems. Divides block designs into five groups: Square and
rectangle, diagonals, open seam, 150 metric shapes and miscellaneous. Discusses template cutting and piecing. Emphasis is on the
block pattern and its assembly. Does not discuss larger items.

112. Hinson, Dolores. A Quilter's Companion. New York: Arco
     Publishing Inc., 1973, 279pp.
         Contains index, directions for 150 pieced and appliquéd
blocks and over fifty border and quilting patterns. Gives full-size
patterns for embroidery, quilting designs, borders and blocks. Black-
and-white illustrations of completed blocks. Suggestions for color
and layout.

113. _____. Quilting Manual. New York: Hearthside Press
     Inc., 1966, 192pp.
         Contains black-and-white drawings by the author of blocks
classified by construction. Examples of quilting patterns, reduced
in size. Examples of borders. Short history of quilts. Forty-
one-item glossary. Index to text and to quilt names.

114. _____. A Second Quilter's Companion. New York: Arco
     Publishing Inc., 1981, 250pp.

Contains index. Over sixty-five block designs, both traditional and modern. Indicates level of difficulty for each project.
For each design, author notes description, directions and gives full-
size patterns. Discusses color, using frames and materials. Chapters on borders; Two, Three and Five-Patch patterns; Four-Patch
patterns; Nine-Patch patterns and quilting patterns. Large black-
and-white sketches of blocks. E.g.: Pinwheel, Potomac Sun and
Spinner. Suggestions for making a quilt top using a specific pattern.

115. Hitchcock, Ruth. A World Of Miniature Quilting. Dunwoody,
      Ga.: By the Author, 1981, 16pp.
            Directions for bed coverings and smaller projects. Color
photos on cover. Projects scaled one inch to one foot. E.g., bed
quilts, pillowcases and cushions.

116. Holland, Nina. Pictorial Quilting. South Brunswick, N. J.:
      A. S. Barnes & Co., 1978, 144pp.
            Includes index, brief bibliography, over 100 black-and-
white photos and sixteen color plates. History of pictorial quilts,
construction directions and a chapter on quilts as fund raisers.
Discusses theme, layout and design, appliqué, embroidery and quilting. Suggestions for fabric and sewing notions. Chapter on local
heritage quilts: Rockport, Maine, Historic Boscasen, N. H., Lyme
Towne, N. H., Birmingham Bloomfield Art Association, Orwell,
Vt., Worcester, Mass., Middlebury, Vt. and numerous others.

117. Holstein, Jonathan. The Pieced Quilt: An American Design
      Tradition. New York: Galahad Books, 1973, 187pp.
            Emphasis is on New England, Pennsylvania and Amish
quilts. Touches on Appalachian, Midwestern and Southern quiltmaking.
Contains index, sixty-six-item bibliography and footnotes. Over 100
color photos, fifty in black and white. Discusses the color and pattern of the pieced quilt design and modern art. Examples of quilts
pictured: Eccentric Star (1910), Mariner's Compass (c. 1820), Joseph's Coat (c. 1890) and Modernistic Tulips (c. 1910).

118. Houck, Carter. Nova Scotia Patchwork Patterns. New York:
      Dover, 1981, 64pp.
            Instructions and full-size patterns for twelve quilts. E.g.,
Nine-Patch quilts, square and triangle variations, Windmill, Basket,
T-Square and Jacob's Ladder. Black-and-white illustration of block
and of the finished quilt. Directions for planning, cutting and con-
struction, with note on the pattern name. Illustrated quilting patterns.
Four pages of introductory material. Color cover.

119. _____. The Patchwork Pattern Book Reworked and Adapted
      for American Quilters from the Japanese Edition. New York:
      E. P. Dutton, 1981, 103pp.
            List of mail-order suppliers in the United States and
Canada. Black-and-white illustrations, color photos of small items,
quilts and wall hangings, with directions. Full-size block patterns
and quilting designs. Gives fabric requirements and finished size
of quilt. Thirty-four traditional American patterns such as Log

Cabin, Double Irish Chain, Shoo Fly and School House. Does not give general directions.

120. _____ . White Work: Techniques and 188 Designs. New
    York: Dover, 1978, 58pp.
        Twenty illustrated stitches. E. g. , Lazy Daisy, French
Knots, Buttonhole, Herringbone, Star and numerous designs.

121. _____ and Miller, Myron. American Quilts and How to
    Make Them. New York: Charles Scribner's Sons, 1979,
    200p.
        Contains index of historic homes and museums showing
quilts; index of quilts and pattern names, list of suppliers. Forty-
two old quilts shown in historic homes or museums, black-and-white
photos and illustrations and color photos. Fifty-seven full-size patterns. Examples of linsey-woolsey, raised white-work (1916), album
quilts, Cockscomb, baby quilts, Whig Rose, Simple Star and Oak
Leaf Cluster. Short history, discussion and photos of early frames.
Instructional chapters on beginning the project and brief section on
care and restoration. History of the various homes mentioned.

122. Ickis, Marguerite. The Standard Book of Quiltmaking and
    Collecting. New York: Greystone Press, 1949; reprint ed.
    Glouster, Mass.: Peter Smith, 1973, 273pp.
        Contains index of almost 200 illustrated block designs--
pieced and appliquéd, black-and-white photos and directions for pattern drafting. Sewing directions for blocks and borders, fabric requirements and quilting suggestions. Some black-and-white illustrations of embroidery stitches. Full-size pattern pieces, e. g. , Twin-
kling Star, Pineapple and Moon Over the Mountain. Examples of
quilting designs: Pineapple, American Eagle (full-size) and all-over
patterns. Discusses borders, appliqué and tufting. Chapter on collecting and the origins of the craft.

123. Illinois Quilters Inc. Prarie Patchwork. Wilmette, Ill.: By
    the Author, 1982, spiral.
        Forty-two modern and traditional patterns relating to
Illinois. Published for the Land of Lincoln Symposium in July 1982.
Both pieced and appliéd patterns for beginners and more advanced
quilters.

124. Imbach, Gay and Bacon, Joyce J. Adventures in Patchwork
    Book I. Corona, Calif.: By the Author, 1982.
        Original patterns for doll, wall and bed quilts and small
projects. Three-, four-, five-, six- and twelve-inch blocks. Color
plates.

125. _____ and _____ . Miniature Magic. Corona, Calif.:
    By the Author, 1981, 96pp.
        Traditional and original patterns for miniature pieced
designs. Over 150 patterns for three-, four-, five-, and six-inch
blocks. Directions. Thirty-seven color photos and fourteen black-
and-white photos. Thirty-four border patterns and quilting designs.
Bibliography.

126. Ives, Suzy. Ideas for Patchwork. Newton Centre, Mass.:
      Charles T. Branford Co., 1974, 112pp.
          Lists suppliers in Great Britain and the United States.
Black-and-white drawings. Briefly discusses tools, fabric, template
construction and color. English method for decorating home items
such as pillow cases, sheets, lamp shades, cushions and tablecloths.
Yardage requirements given in yards and centimeters.

127. James, Michael. The Quiltmakers Handbook: A Guide to De-
      sign and Construction. Englewood Cliffs, N. J.: Prentice-
      Hall Inc., 1978, 147pp.
          Contains index and bibliography. Discusses pieced work
and appliqué. How to quilt and finish the item. Sixteen pages of
color photos. Black-and-white photos and illustrations. Section on
contemporary machine piecing. Short section on the English method
and Seminole technique. Also discusses enlarging patterns, hanging
a quilt and choosing colors. Instructional book.

128. _____. The Second Quiltmakers Handbook: Creative Ap-
      proaches to Contemporary Quilt Designs. Englewood Cliffs,
      N. J.: Prentice-Hall, 1981, 184pp.

          Includes index and bibliography on quilting basics, design,
color and crafts. Thirty-six color plates, numerous black-and-white
photos and illustrations. Photos of quilts created by Nancy Halpern,
Nancy Crow, Maria McCormick-Snyder, Radka Donnell Vogt, Beth
Gutcheon, the author and others. Chapters on the geometry of the
pieced quilt, color, curved seams, strip piecing, the Log Cabin,
surface line and texture. Also discusses care of quilt fabric and
photographing quilts.

129. Jarnow, Jill. The Patchwork Point of View. New York:
      Simon & Schuster, 1975, 157pp.
          Eight-item bibliography, black-and-white illustrations and
color photos. Discusses how to choose fabric, color and supplies.
Technique for patchwork, parallel-strip patchwork, appliqué and crazy
quilting. Examples of clothing, pillows and small ornaments.

130. Johannah, Barbara. Continuous Curve Quilting: Machine Quilt-
      ing the Pieced Quilt. Menlo Park, Calif.: By the Author, 1980,
      56pp.
          Thirty-three patterns for using a figure/ground relation-
ship. Technique for using the sewing machine to move from area
to area without finishing off and starting new threads.

131. _____. The Quick Quiltmaking Handbook. Menlo Park,
      Calif.: By the Author, 1979, 128pp.
          Includes instructions, diagrams and charts to illustrate a
a method for reducing the time needed to construct a quilt. Step-
by-step instructions for squares, rectangles, diamonds, triangles,
Log Cabin and others.

132. Johnson, Mary Elizabeth. Country Quilt Patterns. Birming-
      ham, Ala.: Oxmoor House, 1977, 80pp.

Illustrates twenty-three quilt designs with patterns for block submitted to Progressive Farmer's Country Living Quilt Block Contest. Description and statement by the artist accompanies each block. Includes quilting designs and diagrams; color photos of quilt blocks.

133. _____. Prize Country Quilts. Birmingham, Ala.: Oxmoor House, 1977, 230pp.
Color photos of the fifty blocks designed by winners and runners-up in the Progressive Farmer magazine's second national contest. Includes patterns, techniques, discussion of fabric and color, with a short explanation of the English method. Five pages of embroidery stitches. Short statement by the artist on her original pattern. Twenty-eight-item bibliography.

134. Johnson, Orinne. Quilts: New Patterns and Designs. St. Paul: Webb Publishing Co., 1937; reprint ed., Alanson, Mich.: Barbara Bannister, 1982, 16pp.
From the Farmer's Wife magazine (Book of Quilts No. 4). Ten full-size patterns, including Daisy Star, Tulip Garden, Melon Patch and Orange Peel, with brief directions. Illustrates quilting patterns available from the magazine.

135. _____ and Lewis, Eleanor. The Farmer's Wife Book of New Designs and Patterns. Book No. 3. St. Paul, Minn.: Webb Publishing Co., 1934; reprint ed., Alanson, Mich.: Barbara Bannister, 1978, 17pp.
General instructions for the patterns given. Full-size patterns for sixteen blocks, including Wildwood Wreath, Snow Flake, Waterwheel, Stepping Stones and Fortune's Wheel.

136. _____ and _____. Farmer's Wife Book of Quilts (new edition). St. Paul, Minn.: Webb Publishing Co., 1931; reprint ed., Alanson, Mich.: Barbara Bannister, 1979, 31pp.
Introductory directions on making a quilt. Seventeen full-size patterns including Pine Tree, Double T, Whirligig, and Jacob's Ladder. All accompanied by black-and-white illustration of completed block. Brief instructions for each block. Ideas for quilting designs.

137. _____ and _____. The Farmer's Wife New Book of Quilts. St. Paul: Webb Publishing Co., 1934; reprint ed., Alanson, Mich.: Barbara Bannister, 1979, 31pp.
Cover: Quilts: A New Book of Patterns. Full-size patterns for twelve quilt blocks, both pieced and appliquéd. E.g., Broken Saw, Rising Sun, Greek Puzzle, Primrose and Dogwood. All accompanied by illustration of the finished block. Black-and-white illustration of eighteen additional blocks with no patterns. E.g., Sunbonnet Baby, Rolling Stone, Tea Leaf. General directions and illustrations of quilting patterns (not full-size).

138. Kahn, Barbara. Seminole Patchwork, Principles and Designs. Goshen, N.Y.: Seminole Research/Design Project, 1980, 75pp.

Short history of Seminole Indians. Glossary, construction techniques, black-and-white photos and a bibliography.

139. Kakalia, Kepola. Hawaiian Quilting as an Art: As Instructed by Kepola U. Kakalia. Honolulu, Hawaii: Deborah U. Kakalia, 1976, 40pp.
Chapters on the history of Hawaiian quilting, supplies, fabric and technique. Instructions for a pillow and wall hanging. Chapter on various designs with patterns. How to enlarge and reduce a pattern. Full-size patterns with quilting charts for: Breadfruit, Candle-Lite Tree, Hibiscus, Pineapple, Papaya and Passion Fruit. Black-and-white and color photos of wall hangings and pillows. Black-and-white illustrations of pattern folding and fabric.

140. Khin, Yvonne. The Collector's Dictionary of Quilt Names and Patterns. Washington, D. C.: Acropolis Books, 1980, 489pp.
Patterns categorized according to construction: square, rectangle, diamond, circle, hexagon and appliqué. Index of 2,400 block pattern names, with black-and-white drawings of each. Some color photos. Notes source of pattern: book title and page, columnist or catalog. Twenty-four item glossary, twenty-item bibliography.

141. Ladies Art Company. Quilt Patterns: Patchwork and Applique. St. Louis: Ladies Art Company, 1928; reprint ed., Alanson, Mich.: Barbara Bannister, 1977, 27pp.
General directions for quiltmaking. Pages 5 to 26 illustrate 576 block patterns with name and size of finished block. Illustrates arrangement of eight patterns in a quilt.

142. Lane, Maggie. Maggie Lane's Oriental Patchwork. New York: Charles Scribner's Sons, 1978, 104pp.
Sixteen original patterns for clothing, sixteen color photos, seven-item bibliography. Black-and-white illustrations. Patterns for basic coat, magyar coat, cape, tabard, kite and man's caftan (not full-size). Discussion of Japanese sixteenth-century patchwork, Japanese sampler patchwork and Imari or Tortoise shell (full-size patterns for these). Describes equipment, pattern making, sewing method. Illustrations of reduced patterns on graph paper. Directions.

143. Lane, Rose W. Woman's Day Book of American Needlework. New York: Simon & Schuster, 1963, 208pp.
Chapters on quilts pp. 76 to 123; black-and-white, and color photos of quilts from the Shelburne, the Brooklyn Museum, the Newark Museum, the Maryland Historical Society and the Index of American Design. Black-and-white illustrations of embroidery patterns and stitches pp. 24 to 37. Full-size patterns for patchwork blocks: Mountain Pink and Crown of Thorns. Chapter on appliqué, including directions and color photos of fifteen antique appliqué blocks. Includes Hawaiian appliqué and a pattern for Oakleaf. Notes the history of various patterns. Includes index.

144. Larsen, Judith, L. and Gull, Carol W. The Patchwork Quilt Design and Coloring Book. New York: Butterick Publishing, 1977, 224pp.

Offers design grids, worksheets and charts for fifty traditional and 100 new designs. Directions for enlarging and reducing
patterns. Over 180 color illustrations. Yardage charts and patterns
for squares, rectangles, triangles and parallelograms. Method for
determining fabric for borders and lining. Full-size patterns.
Graphs for Old Tippecanoe, Eight-Pointed Star, Cat's Cradle, Pinwheel and others. Forty-five pages of introductory directions including discussion of design and color.

145. Laury, Jean Ray. New Uses for Old Laces. New York:
     Doubleday, 1974, 109pp.
          Numerous black-and-white photos of lacework applied to
fabric for use in contemporary needlework, including a chapter on
its use in quilts. Illustrates old doilies tacked onto a quilt to give
it an antique block look. Illustrations of embroidery stitches and
quilting techniques.

146. _____. Quilts and Coverlets. A Contemporary Approach.
     New York: Van Nostrand Reinhold Co., 1970, 128pp.
          Modern examples of appliqué, pieced work and quilting.
Sixteen pages of color photos. Also contains black-and-white photos
and illustrations. E. g., Flag quilt, Hills and Valleys, Denim quilt,
American Dream, tie-dyed quilt and a child's quilt.

147. Leman, Bonnie. Quick and Easy Quilting. Great Neck, N. Y.:
     Hearthside Press, 1972, 191pp.
          Includes index and a nine-item bibliography. Step-by-step
instructions with illustrations. Four color plates, black-and-white
illustrations and photos. Twenty-five full-size patterns. E. g., Martha Washington Star, Flower Appliqué, Christmas Tree. Photo of
nineteenth-century Canadian patchwork table cover, novelty quilts,
e. g., biscuit, shadow quilt, cathedral window, puff block, string
quilts and trapunto. Discusses hand and machine embroidery and
quilting on the sewing machine.

148. _____ and Martin, Judy. Log Cabin Quilts. Wheatridge,
     Colo.: Moon Over the Mountain Publishing Co., 1980,
     33pp.
          Forty-eight color photos of antique and modern quilts.
Two hundred diagrams for thirty different Log Cabin blocks. Full-
size patterns. Directions for both hand and machine piecing and
fabric selection. Yardage calculations. Notes history of pattern.

149. _____ and _____. Taking the Math Out of Patchwork
     Quilts. Wheatridge, Colo.: Moon Over the Mountain Publish-
     ing Co., 1981, 36pp.
          Yardage charts, equivalent conversion tables. For ex-
ample, Lone Star and Grandmother's Flower Garden. How to enlarge and reduce patterns. Thirty-six charts in all.

150. Lewis, Alfred A. Mountain Artisans Quilting Book. New York:
     Macmillan Publishing Co., 1973, 179pp.
          Relates the history of the Mountain Artisans quilting

cooperative of West Virginia. Instructions for crazy quilts, Tree of
Life and others. Photos and color illustrations.

151.   Lindsey, Linda.   Cotton Patches: An Outline Notebook for
       Patchwork and Quilting.   Monmouth, Ore.:   By the Author,
       1978, 43pp.
              Includes a course outline and fifty-one-item bibliography.
Discusses history, planning a project, design, cutting, hand and machine sewing, appliqué, piecing, borders, quilting and care of quilted
items.

152.   _____.   Designs for Quilting and Needle Arts.   Monmouth,
       Ore.:   By the Author, 1980, 75pp.
              Ninety-six designs for quilting categorized as curved,
geometric, nature, whimsey, those for children, for the kitchen
and trees.

153.   Lithgow, Marilyn.   Quiltmaking and Quiltmakers.   New York:
       Funk and Wagnalls, 1974, 100pp.
              Includes index and eighteen-item bibliography.   Eight
pages of color photos, black-and-white photos and illustrations.
Seventy-two patterns illustrated and discussed.   E.g., Biblical quilt,
Cottage Tulip, Drunkard's Path and Yankee Puzzle.   Discussion of
pioneer women, quilting auctions and bees, pattern design, quilt
names and stories, fabric and a chapter on making a quilt.

154.   Lobley, Priscilla.   Your Book of Patchwork.   London: Faber
       & Faber, 1974, 75pp.
              Two color photos: nineteenth-century quilt and a Log
Cabin.   Sixteen black-and-white photos.   Numerous illustrations
showing construction technique (English method), color wheel and
geometric patterns.   Brief list of recommended reading, museums
and template suppliers.   Basic introductory chapters on beginning a
quilting project; making templates and using geometric shapes.   Small
projects.   Chapter on "Patchwork in the Past."

155.   McCall's Needlework and Craft Publications.   Bicentennial
       Quilt Book.   New York: McCall's Pattern Co., 1975, 64pp.
              Color photos of twenty-six quilts, many antique examples
of pieced and appliquéd work.   Accompanied by directions, patterns
and a brief statement on the quilt.   Also contains directions for
small items such as a wall hanging, table skirt and a pillow.   Includes list of suppliers.   Pictures of quilts include Bowknots (1900-
1919), Squares (1860-1880), Whirligigs (1860), Missouri Beauty (1880)
and Red Furrows (1935).

156.   _____.   How to Quilt It.   New York: The McCall's Pat-
       tern Co., 1979, 64pp.
              General quilting directions.   Discussion of patchwork,
appliqué, trapunto, biscuit quilts and quilting.   Contains index,
McCall mail-order guide and color photos of quilts such as Lone
Star, Multipattern, Little Red School House, Windmill and Drunkard's Path.   Notes size, equipment needed, fabric requirements and

directions for quilts pictured and for smaller items such as potholders and wall hangings. Black-and-white and color illustrations of block patterns such as Shoo Fly, Pandora's Box, Double Wedding Ring and Pinwheel.

157. _____. The McCall's Book of Quilts. New York: Simon & Schuster/The McCall's Pattern Co., 1975, 157pp.
      Contains an index, general directions, color photos and black-and-white illustrations showing how to construct items such as patchwork quilts, appliqué quilts, pillows, novelty and contemporary quilts and wall hangings. Seventy-seven projects in all. Illustrates quilting designs and seven embroidery stitches. Notes the finished quilt size, fabric and directions. Some of the full-size patterns given include Rose of Sharon, Eagle, Kentucky Rose, Whig Rose, Clamshell and Triangles.

158. _____. McCall's Needlework Treasury: A Learn and Make Book. New York: Random House, 1964, 390pp.
      Section on quilting pp. 95 to 132. Black-and-white and color photos; color illustrations. Chapters on appliqué San Blas appliqué, pieced work, trapunto and candlewicking. Directions on how to copy an old quilt, noting size, equipment and materials needed. Short discussion on the evolution of patchwork. Contains index and quilting patterns.

159. _____. McCall's Quilting, Patchwork and Applique Encyclopedia: A Learn by Doing Book, Vol. 4. New York: The McCall's Pattern Co., 1978, 192pp.
      Contains index, a list of suppliers, and a twenty-seven-item glossary. Discusses how to enlarge, reduce, and construct a pattern. Examples of twenty-five embroidery stitches. Color photos, black-and-white illustrations and patterns, not all full-size. Directions on how to make the quilts shown, such as a Victorian wall hanging, Rob Peter to Pay Paul, Pineapple, Bed of Flowers and Calico Cat and Gingham Dog. Also gives directions for pillows and a tablecloth.

160. _____. McCall's Super Book of Quilting. New York: ABC Needlework and Crafts Magazines, 1976, 153pp.
      Color photos of traditional and modern quilts. Some full-size patterns. E. g., Radical Rose, Eagle, Plume and Mariner's Compass. Instructions for making each quilt shown, including Pine Tree, Baskets, Irish Chain, Stars, Whig Rose and Rose of Sharon.

161. McClosky, Marsha. Small Quilts. Bothell, Wash. : That Patchwork Place Inc., 1982, 48pp.
      Illustrations, black-and-white and color photos. Metric conversion chart and bibliography. Directions for eight machine-pieced quilts: Puss in the Corner, Jacob's Ladder, Sister's Choice, Melon Patch, Snowball, Churn Dash, Rising Star and Turkey Tracks.

162. MacDonald, Jessie and Shaefer, Marion H. Let's Make A Patchwork Quilt Using a Variety of Sampler Blocks. Philadelphia: Speciality Books, 1980, 128pp.

Introduction to terminology. Yardage charts, full-size
patterns, color photos of finished quilts and single blocks. E. g.,
Shoo Fly, Greek Cross, Churn Dash, Jacob's Ladder and Ohio Star.
Directions for smaller projects such as pillows. Chapter on appliqué
accompanied by patterns. Directions for quilting and assembly. Also
illustrates stitches.

163. McIntyre, Ione B. American History in Patchwork Patterns:
      The Charter Oak. Vol. 1. Bemidji, Minn.: The Patchwork
      Press, 1981, 52pp.
           Black-and-white illustrations of completed block, various
renditions of the Charter Oak pattern. Gives sources of patterns
and short histories. Color photos of completed quilts. Full-size
patterns for tracing. Fifty-four-item bibliography.

164. McKain, Sharon. The Great Noank Quilt Factory: How to
      Make Quilts and Quilted Things. New York: Random House,
      1974, 136pp.
           Full-size patterns for Rose of Sharon, Hawaiian, Dresden
Plate and Little House quilts. Basic book with explanations for beginners. Examples of puff quilt, crazy, tied quilt, cathedral window,
strip, Log Cabin, yo-yo, Little House and reverse appliqué. Directions for cutting, sewing and making borders. Step-by-step lessons
for pillows, coats and wall hangings. Color photos of finished items.
Black-and-white illustrations. Sixty-two-item bibliography.

165. McKendry, Ruth. Traditional Quilts and Bed Coverings. New
      York: Van Nostrand Reinhold, 1979, 240pp.
           Published in Canada under the title: Quilts and Other
Bed Coverings in the Canadian Tradition. Text accompanied by color
and black-and-white photos, footnotes, bibliography and index. Discusses quilting from its beginnings to the Victorian era. Relates the
environment of Upper Canada to the craft, discussing various kinds
of quilts and pattern names. Chapters on fabric, borders and batting,
symbols and styles. Also contains glossary.

166. McKim, Lynn and Tittle, Phyllis. Designs Worth Doing. In-
      dependence, Mo.: Acorn Publishing Co., 1979, 120pp.
           Forty-eight full size pattern designs by Ruby McKim.
Pieced, some with appliqué. Directions for the Three Little Pigs
quilt, originally published in 1930.

167. McKim, Ruby. One Hundred and One Patchwork Patterns.
      Independence, Mo.: McKim Studios, 1938; reprint ed., New
      York: Dover, 1962, 124pp.
           Subtitle: Quilt Name Stories, Cutting Designs, Material
Suggestions, Yardage Estimates, Definite Instructions for Every Step
of Quilt Making. Black-and-white illustrations and full-size patterns
for blocks such as: Dresden Flowers, Rose, Pansy appliqué, Butterfly quilt, Palm Leaf and string quilt. Directions for cutting and
choosing fabric, settings, borders and embroidery. Patterns originally published in the Kansas City Star.

168.   McNeill, Moyra. Quilting. London: Octopus Books, 1980,
       80pp.
              Contains color photos and an index; lists suppliers in the
United States and England. Color illustrations, brief history of quilting in Europe, America and Wales. Notes materials needed and
technique. Projects: tea cozy, pillows, appliqué picture, Christening
quilt, clothing and a wall hanging. Discusses English (wadded) quilting, Italian (corded) quilting, using the machine, shadow quilting and
sprayed quilting. No full-size patterns.

169.   _____. Quilting for Today. London: Mills and Boon, 1975,
       64pp.
              Illustrations of stitches and techniques such as English,
trapunto, Italian and shadow. Four pages of color photos; also black-
and-white photos. Illustrations of contemporary wall hangings and
panels, a footstool, stuffed work; no specific directions. General
directions for an altar frontal.

170.   Mahler, Celine B. Once Upon a Quilt: Patchwork Design and
       Technique. New York: Van Nostrand Reinhold Co., 1973, 96pp.
              Author shows patchwork patterns popular from the mid-
nineteenth century to the early 1930's. Seventeen-item glossary.
Black-and-white photos of quilts with title, date and owner's name.
Black-and-white illustrations. Seventeen quilts shown in color. Instructions for hand and machine piecing. Photos of potholders, placemats and pillows. Brief list of suppliers.

171.   Mainardi, Patricia. Quilts: The Great American Art. San
       Pedro, Calif.: R & E Miles, 1979, 57pp.
              Discusses history of quilting up to the present day. Cat-
egorizes quilts by their purpose. Eleven black-and-white photos.
First published in the Feminist Art Journal (Winter 1973).

172.   Major, Connie. Contemporary Patchwork Quilts: A Stitch in
       Our Time. New York: Sterling Publishing Co., 1982, 128pp.
              For the experienced quilter. Chapters on design, color,
patterns and personalizing quilts. Brief directions on how to make
the designs shown. E.g.: Cloverleaf Express, Bicycle Wheels,
Save the Whales and Red Tape. Also contains general directions on
quiltmaking. Thirty-one pages of color photos; black-and-white illustrations and photos. Index, metric equivalency charts.

173.   Malone, Maggie. Classic American Patchwork Quilt Patterns.
       New York: Drake Publishers Inc., 1977, 192pp.
              Illustrates a collection of over 100 traditional pieced block
patterns. Contains index of pattern names and a bibliography. Where
possible, the author gives the earliest date known for each pattern
with background information (history, legends). Each pattern cross-
referenced to show its various names. E.g., Battle of the Alamo,
Beggar Block, Cut Glass Dish, Prairie Queen. Each block annotated
with quilt size, block size, number of blocks in quilt, fabric requirements and brief piecing instructions. Not an instructional book. Full-
size patterns.

174. _____. 1001 Patchwork Designs. New York: Sterling
      Publishing Co., 1982, 224pp.
         Patterns categorized as: one- and two-patch designs,
nine-patch designs, four-patch designs, five-patch designs (hexa-
grams, circles, diamonds and stars) and seven-patch designs. Discusses how to determine quilt size and fabric requirements, quilting
and setting the blocks. Index of pattern names, pp. 219 to 224. Includes metric equivalence chart, black-and-white drawings of the patterns with name (no source or date); chapter on color and a bibliography.

175. Mann, Kathleen. Applique Design and Method. London: A & C
      Black Ltd., 1937, 48pp.
         Black-and-white illustrations and photos, color frontispiece.
Emphasis on wall decoration with illustrations of some stitches. Examples of stuffed toys and a lampshade. Discusses felt appliqué using the inlay technique. Shows appliqué sampler: The Tea Shop.

176. Marston, Doris. Exploring Patchwork. New York: Double-
      day, 1971, 66pp.
         Includes index, brief list of suppliers and a bibliography.
Black-and-white illustrations and diagrams, black-and-white photos
of finished projects. E.g., pillows, boxes, tea cozy, tote bag,
clothing and bed quilts. Chapters on the clamshell, triangles, patchwork clothing and quilts. Discussion of modern trends and ideas.

177. _____. Patchwork Today: A Practical Introduction. New-
      ton Centre, Mass.: Charles T. Branford, 1968, 92pp.
         Contains index, short list of books and English suppliers.
Sixteen pages of photos of contemporary items including wall hanging, pillow and tea cozy. Chapter on the hexagon, diamond, clamshell and pentagon, octagon and long diamond. English method of
combining shapes, Instructional book emphasizing geometric designs.

178. Martin, Judy. Patchworkbook: Easy Lessons for Creative
      Quilt Design and Construction. New York: Charles Scribner's
      Sons, 1983, 169pp.
         Contains index of pattern names, black-and-white and
color illustrations of quilt blocks. Twelve color photos of quilts
such as Angel's Flight, Wheel of Fortune and Barrister's Block,
accompanied by description. Instructional book emphasizing block
design, setting the blocks and borders. Each chapter concludes with
an exercise for testing skills. Formula for figuring quilt size and
yardage. Sewing tips.

179. Martins, Rachel. Modern Patchwork. New York: Doubleday,
      1971, 56pp.
         Emphasis is on design, with color illustrations. Block
patterns from Farm Journal of the 1920's, shown for modern use.
Illustrates placemats, beach bag, skirt, bedspread and table runner.
Full-size patterns, e.g., Kings' Cross, Twelve Triangles, Starry
Path, Peaceful Hours and Formal Garden. Color photo of child's
quilt. Idea book, no detailed instructions.

180.   Mattera, Joanne, ed.   The Quiltmaker's Art: Contemporary
       Quilts and Their Makers.   Asheville, N. C.:   Lark Books,
       1982, 132pp.
              Ninety photos of modern quilts, including over fifty-five
color plates.   Two-page bibliography.   Biographical information on
the quilters, annotated with their addresses, photograph, where they
have exhibited and what publications have documented their work.
Photos of the work of artists such as Nancy Crow, Michael James,
Charlotte Pattera, Jody Klein, Patsy Allen and David Hornung, with
their comments.   Black-and-white photo of Harriet Powers' Bible
quilt (c. 1895-98), with a short biography of the artist.   Quilt photos
noted with title, year, materials used and size of quilt.

181.   Meeker, L. K.   Quilt Patterns for the Collector with Keys for
       Drafting.   Portland, Ore.:   By the Author, 1979, 56pp.
              A catalog method for the pattern collector, with directions
on using the system.

182.   Miles, Elaine and Peace and Plenty Quilting Society.   Many
       Hands: Making a Communal Quilt.   San Pedro, Calif.:   R & E
       Miles, 1982, 74pp.
              Instructions for making a communal baby quilt that can
be applied to any group quilt.   Discusses choosing a coordinator,
designing the quilt, fabric requirements and assembling the top.
Also contains full-size patterns for the ten-inch and six-inch blocks
of the baby quilt.   Directions and quilting designs.

183.   Miller, Stephanie.   Creative Patchwork.   New York: Crown,
       1971, 96pp.
              Introductory chapters on patchwork, hexagons, how to
make a coat, a poncho, triangles and diamonds, combined shapes,
clamshell, cathedral window, suffolk puffs and padded work.   Section
on design, color and texture.   Section on traditional patchwork designs; eighteen black-and-white illustrations with descriptions.   Two
color illustrations: Dresden Plate and Virginia Star.   Discusses
alternate quilt names.   Black-and-white illustrations of Moon Over
the Mountain, Roman Square, Grandmothers Fan, Rob Peter to
Pay Paul and Flying Geese; color photos of Sawtooth Star, Snowflake,
Schoolhouse, Ohio Farmyard and Meadow Lily.   Discusses Victorian
patchwork, contemporary work, toys and pictorial quilts.

184.   Mills, Susan W.   Illustrated Index to Traditional American
       Quilt Patterns.   New York: Arco Publishing Inc., 1980, 124pp.
              An index of over 700 block patterns, a twenty-four-item
bibliography and a foreword.   Black-and-white illustrations of the
patterns, with their various names.   Includes stars, triangles, circles, combinations, rectangles and octagons, hexagons and diamonds.

185.   Mitchell, Jean.   Quilt Kansas!   Lawrence, Kan.:   By the
       Author, 1978, 40pp.
              Prepared for the 1978 Kansas Quilt Symposium.   Forty
full-size patterns using Kansas as a theme.   Accompanied by block
illustration, description and background; some by Carrie Hall, Rose

Kretsinger, Scioto I. Danner and the author. E.g., Kansas Troubles, Kansas Beauty, Kansas Rose, Emporia Rose and Sunflower.

186.   Morgan, Mary and Mosteller, Dee. Trapunto and Other Forms of Raised Quilting. New York: Charles Scribner's Sons, 1977, 218pp.
        Extensive list of suppliers. Full-size patterns, black-and-white photos and illustrations; two-page glossary. Chapters on the origins of trapunto, contemporary work and utilizing the design. Photos and illustrations of the stitches used in quilting. Discusses raising the design, stuffing, cording, raised appliqué and special techniques. Section on teaching children how to do trapunto, care and cleaning of fabric and making special projects such as pillows, wall hangings, clothing and small household items.

187.   Munkelwitz, Kathleen. The I've Never Made a Quilt Before Quilt Book. Isle, Minn.: By the Author, 1980, 56pp.
        Contains fourteen pieced patterns, quilting designs and directions. Discusses fabric, quilting and the technique of tying. Patterns include Clay's Choice, Stepping Stones, Maple Leaf and Sunflower.

188.   Museum of Fine Arts, Boston. A Pattern Book Based on an Appliquéd Quilt by Mrs. Harriet Powers, American, 19th Century. Boston: Museum of Fine Arts, 1973, 32pp.
        Reduced patterns for fifteen blocks of a Harriet Powers quilt made between 1895 and 1898. Each block accompanied by captions written by Mrs. Powers. Some blocks shown: Block 1: Job Praying for his Enemies; 2: Dark Day of May 19, 1780 and 3: Serpent lifted up by Moses. Line drawings of figures in the quilts reduced 58 percent. Color photo of quilt on the cover.

189.   Nelson, Cyril and Houck, Carter. The Quilt Engagement Calendar Treasury. New York: E. P. Dutton, 1982, 272pp.
        Compilation of quilt photos published in The Quilt Engagement Calendar from 1975 to 1982, and some new ones. Color photo from the exhibit: Ohio Quilts: A Living Tradition, showing the collection of Darwin Bearley and from the show Baltimore Album Quilts. Color plates of full-size quilts pp. 5-186, 185 plates in all. Annotation gives type of construction, date, size, short description of the quilt, history of showings, if known, and the owner's name; also gives plate numbers for similar quilts. Pictures of all types of quilts--antique and contemporary. Full-size patterns and instructions for twenty-one quilts shown. List of mail-order sources and a brief bibliography. Instructions include illustration of finished quilt with reference to color plate number, fabric requirements, dimensions, cutting and piecing directions and block sketches for Mariner's Compass, Johnny Round the Corner, Road to California, Blossoms and Berries, Pineapple, Touching Stars, Barn Raising and others.

190.   Newman, Thelma. Quilting Patchwork Appliqué and Trapunto: Traditional Methods and Original Designs. New York: Crown, 1974, 248pp.

Contains eight pages of color photos, numerous black-and-white photos and illustrations and an index. List of supply sources, pp. 241-245; glossary, pp. 235-238. Discusses background information, starting the design, choosing color and fabric. Chapters on machine work, tying and care of quilts. Patchwork technique and appliqué, Hawaiian and mola technique, banners and new directions in quilting. Discusses three-dimensional work: stuffed, trapunto, corded and forms in the round. Photo annotations give size, artist, brief description and museum where item can be seen. Lengthy section on modern work. Examples from the Connecticut Historical Society, Kauai Museum, Smithsonian Institution, Charleston Museum, the Shelburn, Victoria and Albert Museum and the Metropolitan Museum of Art.

191. Nield, Dorothea. Adventures in Patchwork. London: Mills
     and Boon Ltd., 1975, 84pp.
             Emphasis is on pattern design. Chapters on diamonds, box patterns, use of printed fabric, embroidery and Seminole. Color and black-and-white photos. List of suppliers and a brief bibliography. Lists places to see patchwork in England, Scotland, the United States and Bermuda.

192. Orbelo, Beverly. A Texas Quilting Primer. 3rd ed. San
     Antonio, Tex.: Corona Publishing Co., 1981, 45pp.
             Forty-seven patterns relating to Texas. Notes their history. Bibliography. E.g., Battle of the Alamo, Chisholm Trail, Texas Bluebonnet and Tumbleweed. Patterns geared for beginner, intermediate and advanced quilters.

193. Orlofsky, Patsy and Orlofsky, Myron. Quilts in America.
     New York: McGraw-Hill, 1974, 368pp.
             Historical overview of quilts up to the twentieth century. Bibliography and index. Lists museums having quilts for viewing. Forty-eight color pages. Over 300 illustrations. Also discusses care of quilts.

194. Parker, Kay. Contemporary Quilts: Original Patterns Based
     on the Drawings of M. C. Escher. Trumansburg, N.Y.: The
     Crossing Press, 1981, 128pp.
             Color cover, four pages of color photos of quilts. Patterns for eight designs. Illustrated instructions for twenty-one projects. Chapter on adapting the new design to pieced work. The designs consist of figures and animals in a repeat pattern. Lists sources. Some patterns: arrows, sea turtles, mosaic, reptiles, birds, fish and whales. Instructions for creating your own design.

195. Patera, Charlotte. The Applique Book. New York: Creative
     Home Library, 1974, 264pp.
             Discusses color, fabric selection, enlarging designs, gluing, framing and caring for quilts. Eight techniques and thirteen items for boutique or bazaar. Examples and directions for pillows, chair seats, a room divider and caftan. Holiday and seasonal ideas

for a hex, table runner and placemats.   Color photos, black-and-white illustrations and bibliography.

196. _____. The Mola Pattern Book.   Novato, Calif.:   By the
       Author, 1979, 23pp.
              Directions and ten full-size patterns for two styles of
molas.   Diagrams and bibliography.

197. _____. The Stained Glass Pattern Book for Reverse Appli-
       qué.   Novato, Calif.:   By the Author, 1980, 24pp.
              Instructions with sixteen patterns.   Black-and-white illus-
trations.

198. Payne, Suzzy and Murwin, Susan.   Creative American Quilting
       Inspired by the Bible.   Old Tappan, N. J.:   Fleming H. Revell
       Co., 1983, 175pp.
              Ten patterns with a biblical theme.   Illustrated.

199. Peto, Florence.   American Quilts and Coverlets.   New York:
       Chanticleer Press, 1949, 63pp.
              Discussion of quilts made between 1748 and 1800; 1800
and 1840; 1840 and 1948; with a chapter on woven coverlets.   Part
Two discusses how to make a quilt: material, cutting, piecing and
appliqué, with patterns such as Four-Patch, Grandmothers Flower
Garden, Six-Point Star and Star of LeMoyne.   Also covers borders,
quilting and binding.   Photos of old-fashioned sewing items: brass
sewing bird (clamp), printing block, pin cushion, spool and reel.
Fourteen-item bibliography, fifty patterns and diagrams, fifty-six
photos in color and black-and-white.

200. _____. Historic Quilts.   New York: American Historical
       Co., 1939, 210pp.
              Sixty-one plates.   Author writes of her philosophy that
quilts reflect the times and place of their creation.

201. Pforr, Effie C.   Award Winning Quilts.   Birmingham, Ala.:
       Oxmoor House, 1974, 184pp.
              List of award winners and honorable mentions from Pro-
gressive Farmer's Quilt Block contest.   Background on the social
significance of quilts.   Part One: Color photos of historic quilts.
Part Two: Discusses how to make a quilt, illustrated with color
photos showing cutting, piecing and quilting.   Part Three: Contest
winners; color photos of traditional and contemporary pattern blocks
with description, pattern name, winner's name, city/state and a short
statement.   Bibliography, pp. 182-183.   Sixty patterns in all.

202 Porcella, Yvonne.   Pieced Clothing.   Modesto, Calif.:   By the
       Author, 1981, 40pp.
              Color cover, eight pages of color photos.   Directions
for making fourteen items of clothing.   Discusses cutting and measuring.

203. _____. Pieced Clothing Variations.   Modesto, Calif.:   By
       the Author, 1981, 40pp.

Color cover, twelve color photos of clothing.   Directions
for making ten garments (vest, jackets, etc.) using one basic pattern.

204.   Puckett, Marjorie.   Patchwork Possibilities.   Orange, Calif.:
By the Author, 1982, 100pp.
One hundred seventy black-and-white illustrations, twenty-
one color plates, forty full-size patterns.   Discusses crazy quilts,
appliqué and piecing, how to bind and hang a quilt.

205.   _____.   String Quilts 'n Things.   Orange, Calif.:   By the
Author, 1979, 61pp.
Sixty-four color plates, illustrating step-by-step directions.   Discusses fabric selection and color.   Ideas for gifts, home
accessories and clothing.   Patterns.

206.   _____ and Giberson, Gail.   Primarily Patchwork.   Orange,
Calif.:   By the Authors, 1975, 100pp.
Instructions for small items and quilts.   Full-size patterns for forty-two pieced designs.   One hundred color plates.   Be-
gins with small projects that lead into quilts.   Illustrations.

207.   Reader's Digest Association.   Complete Guide to Needlework.
Pleasantville, N. Y.:   The Reader's Digest Assn., 1979, 504pp.
Chapters on quilting pp. 191-268.   Instructions on appliqué, including reverse appliqué, patchwork, quilting and projects
such as man's vest, baby quilt, wall hanging, floor pillow and evening bag.   Color photos and illustrations depicting the projects as they
near completion.   How to estimate quilt size, use color and construct a quilting frame.   Also discusses quilting designs, machine
quilting, tying padding, cording and care of quilts.

208.   Rehmel, Judy.   Key to 1000 Quilt Patterns.   Richmond, Ind.:
By the Author, 1978, 240pp.

209.   _____.   Key to a Second 1000 Quilt Patterns.   Richmond,
Ind.:   By the Author, 1978, 240pp.

210.   _____.   Key to a Third 1000 Quilt Patterns.   Richmond,
Ind.:   By the Author, 1980, 240pp.

211.   _____.   Key to a Fourth 1000 Quilt Patterns.   Richmond,
Ind.:   By the Author, 1983, 240pp.
This four-volume set of loose-leaf books is 5-1/2 x 7-3/4
inches.   It has an index and each block is illustrated.   No duplication of patterns.   Organized by categories.

212.   Risinger, Hettie.   Innovative Machine Quilting.   New York:
Sterling Publishing Co., 1980, 160pp.
Contains index, list of suppliers, glossary and tools
needed.   Fabric requirements for quilts shown.   Basic machine
sewing for squares and rectangles, diamonds, rhomboids, hexagons,
octagons, curves, embroidery, appliqué and trapunto.   Discusses
quilting in a small amount of space and the quilt-as-you-go-method.

Shows Seminole and Hawaiian work, cathedral window and how to
figure yardage. Four pages of color photos, black-and-white and
color illustrations.

213.   Robertson, Elizabeth W.   American Quilts.   New York: The
       Studio Publications, Inc., 1948, 152pp.
              Discussion of history of quiltmaking, quilt names and
fabric.   Photos and illustrations of old quilts.   Contains bibliography.

214.   Robinson, Sharon.   Contemporary Quilting.   Worcester, Mass.:
       Davis Publications, 1982, 120pp.
              Includes soft sculpture and use of nonfabric materials.
Various quilting techniques discussed.   Four pages of color photos
and a bibliography.   Illustrates quilts by Nancy Crow, Nancy Halpern
and Jeff Gutcheon.   Directions for Seminole, Hawaiian and yo-yo.

215.   Rose. H. W.   Quilting with Strips and Strings.   New York:
       Dover, 1983, 48pp.
              How to make quilts from leftover fabric.   Forty-six ex-
amples, thirty-one full-size patterns.

216.   Rush, Beverly and Wittman, Lassie.   The Complete Book of
       Seminole Patchwork.   Seattle, Wash.:   Madrona Publishers,
       1982, 132pp.
              Directions, history of Seminole patchwork, black-and-
white and color photos.   Patterns.

217.   Safford, Carlton L. and Bishop, Robert.   America's Quilts
       and Coverlets.   New York: E. P. Dutton, 1972, 313pp.
              Contains index, fifty-nine-item bibliography, over 100
color photos and over 400 black-and-white photos from public and
private collections.   Emphasis on patchwork and appliqué.   Other
coverlets discusses: bed rugs, linsey-woolsey, whole cloth, crewel
spreads, white-work, candlewick, crazies and modern examples of
patchwork and appliqué.   Photos of quilts from the Metropolitan Museum of Art, Henry Ford Museum, Winterthur Museum, Philadelphia
Museum of Art, Newark Museum and numerous others.

218.   Santa Clara Valley Quilt Assn.   I'd Rather Be Quilting.   4 vols.
       Campbell, Calif.:   By the Author, 1977-1982.
              Patterns done by this quilting group.   Pieced and appliquéd.
Brief directions.   Book I: fifty-one patterns, sixty-seven pages;
Book II: forty-six patterns, sixty-nine pages; Book III: forty patterns, sixty-four pages; Book IV: forty-nine patterns, sixty-nine
pages.

219.   Schoenfeld, Susan and Bendiner, Winifred.   Pattern Designs
       for Needlepoint and Patchwork.   New York: Van Nostrand
       Reinhold Co., 1974, 199pp.
              Examples of designs from the Alhambra and Italian fres-
coes.   Text encourages reader to create original designs using pattern sheets (even and odd numbered squares, equilateral triangle and
circle.   Chapter Ten (pp. 170-196) devoted to patchwork.   Photos of

quilts from the Brooklyn Museum and the Metropolitan Museum of Art. Directions for using pattern sheets, patchwork technique, appliqué and quilting. Thirty-five color photos. Over 150 photos in all.

220. Sexton, Carlie. Early American Quilts. Southampton, N. Y.: Cracker Barrel Press, 1924, 16pp.
    Black-and-white photos of blocks, quilts and a quilting bee. Examples of True Lovers Knot, Baby Bunting, Rob Peter to Pay Paul, Dutch Rose and Cherry. Many old patterns, both pieced and appliquéd. Discusses old quilts, borders and quilting. E.g., Set of borders and Democratic Victory, no date. Four line poem by the author.

221. _____. How To Make a Quilt. Privately printed. reprint ed., Alanson, Mich.: Barbara Bannister, n.d., 8pp.
    Instructional pamphlet. Discusses fabric, material needed, joining blocks, appliqué, color, lining, interlining and quilting frames. Black-and-white illustration of a quilting frame. Old photo of a quilting bee.

222. _____. Old Fashioned Quilts. Wheaton, Ill.: By the Author, 1928, reprint ed., Alanson, Mich.: Barbara Bannister, 1964, 24pp.
    Many photos of quilts and quilt blocks. Essays on old quilts the author has seen and on quiltmaking. Examples of blocks: Rose Tree, Prairie Flower, Farmer's Wife, Ohio Rose, Daisy, Turkey Track, Morning Star, Pineapple and Rose Sprig.

223. _____. Yesterday's Quilts in Homes of Today. Des Moines, Iowa: By the Author, 1930; reprint ed., Alanson, Mich.: Barbara Bannister, 1964, 12pp.
    Essay on old quilts, pattern names and quiltmaking, accompanied by black-and-white photos of quilts and blocks. E.g., Baby Rose, Wedding Ring, Oregon Trail and Sunburst.

224. Share, Majorie. Bee Quilting: A Kit for Making Your Own Quilt. Washington, D.C.: Smithsonian Institution Traveling Exhibition Service, 1979. Four brochures.
    For ages twelve and up. Illustrated with instructions and patterns. Written for children.

225. Shipley Art Gallery, Gateshead, England. Patchwork in the North East. Gateshead, Eng.: Tyne and Wear County Council Museum, n.d., 4pp.
    Information sheet on patchwork with thirteen black-and-white photos of quilts. E.g., Levan's Hall quilt, Medallion quilt by "Joe the Quilter" (c. 1800), Star Quilt (c. 1910), strippy quilt and Mosaic.

226. _____. Quilting in the North East. Gateshead, Eng.: Tyne and Wear County Council Museum, n.d., 4pp.
    Information sheet giving brief overview of the subject.

Seven black-and-white photos of quilted items. Two black-and-white illustrations; quilting patterns and Joe the Quilter's cottage.

227.   Short, Eirian. Introducing Quilting. New York: Charles
       Scribner's Sons, 1974, 88pp.
            Lists suppliers in Great Britain and the United States.
Color and black-and-white photos. Many illustrations. Discusses
wadded quilting (tied and lap), flat, corded, stuffed, shadow, gathered, sewing by hand, or on the machine, raised patchwork (Swiss
patchwork), overlapping scales and obtaining a quilted effect with no
stitching.

228.   Solvit, Marie-Janine. Pictures in Patchwork. New York:
       Sterling Publishing Co., 1977, 112pp.
            Photographs from Elle magazine, originally published in
France under the title Le Patchwork by Dessain et Toira, Paris,
1976. Contains index, black-and-white illustrations, over fifty color
photos from Elle magazine. Works from the Golden Needles Exhibit
sponsored by Elle magazine in 1975. Chapter on knitted and cro-
cheted patchwork and hanging a panel. Photos from French quilt
collections.

229.   Sterns & Foster Co. Catalog of Quilt Pattern Designs and Nee-
       dlecraft Supplies. Cincinnati: Stearns & Foster, n.d., 72pp.
            Catalog of pieced, appliquéd and quilting patterns avail-
able from the Stearns & Foster Company. Brief directions for making a quilt or tied comforter. Section on caring for quilts and com-
forters. One hundred and thirty black-and-white illustrations of full
quilts utilizing each of the available patterns, accompanied by a brief
description including finished size. E.g., Tree of Paradise, Harrison Rose, New York Beauty, Dogwood, Pennsylvania Tulip, Wild
Ducks, Floral Cameo, Sea Wings to Glory and Columbine.

230.   Strobl-Wohlschlager, Ilse. Fun with Appliqué and Patchwork.
       New York: Watson-Guptill, 1970, 56pp.
            Color and black-and-white photos of finished items with
brief directions. Indicates kind of fabric needed and gives a short
description of the finished item. No patterns. Idea book for wall
hangings, aprons, table runners and bags.

231.   Svennas, Elsie. Advanced Quilting. New York: Charles
       Scribner's Sons, 1980, 143pp.
            Contains index, sixteen pages of color photos; black-and-
white photos on every page of the book. Also has black-and-white
illustrations. Introductory chapters on quilting, fabric, using the
sewing machine, marking patterns and sewing pieces. Projects:
clothing and accessories, household items and appliqué. Examples
and ideas for contemporary work in three dimensions, quilt patterns
taken from decorative design in ceramics, architecture, leaded win-
dows, stuffed work and modern art. Holiday items, e.g., Christmas Tree, Easter Hens and wreaths. Examples of work from Thai-
land, the Cuna Indians, Hawaii, and Mexico. Examples of toys,
masks, books, quilting and stuffed braille.

232. _____. Patchcraft: Design, Materials, Technique. New
      York: Van Nostrand Reinhold Co., 1972, 96pp.
            Contains index, black-and-white photos. Chapters on
pentagons, hexagons, quadrangles, triangles, rhomboids and irregular
shapes. Discusses quilting, painterly technique and appliqué. Examples: potholders, skirt, pillows, curtains, and creative examples
of appliqué. No patterns.

233. Swan, Susan B. Plain and Fancy: American Women and
      Their Needlework, 1700-1850. New York: Holt, Rinehart and
      Winston, 1977, 240pp.
            Emphasizes the social history of women and their needle-
work. Uses primary sources. Contains glossary, annotated bibliography and index. Forty-two color photos. Over 100 black-and-white
photos.

234. Taylor, Sibby. New and Easy Quilting. New York: A. S.
      Barnes and Co., 1977, 112pp.
            Includes index, bibliography, color and black-and-white
photos. Complete directions for tabletop quilting, planning, Hawaiian
quilting, novelties and restorations. Photos of finished designs:
Basket Weave, Crosspatch, Shoo Fly and Poplar Leaf. Color photo
of child's album quilt. Full-size patterns. Black-and-white photo
of quilt in progress.

235. Timmins, Alice. Introducting Patchwork. New York: Watson-
      Guptill, 1968, 95pp.
            Discusses equipment, materials, templates, color, various
geometric designs and doing patchwork on the sewing machine. How
to make small items such as mobiles, boxes, placemats and a tea
cozy. Lists English suppliers. Black-and-white illustrations and
fifty photos. Eight color pages.

236. _____. Patchwork Simplified. New York: Arco Publish-
      ing, 1973, 96pp.
            Illustrates the English method of sewing fabric over paper
to make modern quilts and smaller projects. Lists suppliers in the
United States and Great Britain. Fifteen-item bibliography. Color
and black-and-white photos. Part One devoted to instructions. Part
Two shows examples of pincushions, placemats, tea cozy, bags,
mobile, panel and bedhead. Chapter on machine sewing. Brief
directions for each item. Some patterns.

237. _____. Patchwork Technique and Design. London: B. T.
      Batsford Ltd., 1980, 144pp.
            Contains index, brief bibliography and a list of suppliers
in England. Black-and-white photos and illustrations. Four pages
of color photos. E. g., dress, quilt and wall hanging. Illustrates
the English method of using paper to prepare patches. Examples
and directions for Log Cabin, Shell, Suffolk Puffs, Dresden Plate
and Seminole. Examples of bags, pillows, and mosaic patchwork
with irregular shapes.

238. Tinkham, Sandra S. , ed. Consolidated Catalog to the Index
      of American Design. Teaneck, N. J. : Somerset House, 1980,
      unpged.
         This catalog lists each object in the Index, with date of
manufacture, materials used, name of the maker, place of origin,
location where it was rendered, date of rendering, artist's name,
the IAD accession number and the microfiche location number. The
microfiche edition of the Index is divided into ten parts, including
textiles. The Index itself is a compilation done during the 1930's
that ended in 1942. Its purpose was to create pictures (renderings)
of American decorative and folk art from the time of settlement to
about 1900. The Index is housed at the National Gallery of Art in
Washington, D. C.

239. Uncoverings: The Research Papers of the American Quilt
      Study Group. Mill Valley, Calif. : AQSG, 1980-
         An annual volume devoted to quilt study and research,
edited by Sally Garoutte. Most articles accompanied by photos and/
or illustrations. Volume 1: 76 pages; Volume 2: 112 pages; Volume 3: 136 pages.

240. Vogue Guide to Patchwork and Quilting. New York: Stein and
      Day, 1973, 80pp.
         An idea book for patchwork and quilting using the English
method of folding fabric over paper. Examples of hexagons, squares
and cord quilting. Items to make: shawl with fabric requirements
and brief directions; pinafore dress; bed jacket; bedspread; jacket.
Black-and-white photos and illustrations, including items from the
Victoria and Albert Museum. Color photo inside covers.

241. Vote, Marjean. Patchwork Pleasure: A Pattern Identification
      Guide. Des Moines: Wallace-Homestead Book Co., n. d. , 83pp.
         Black-and-white photos of fifteen appliqué and sixty-nine
pieced blocks. Short discussion of patchwork terminology and quilt
construction.

242. Webster, Marie. Quilts: Their Story and How to Make Them.
      Garden City, N. Y. : Doubleday Page & Co. , 1915, 178pp.
         Contains list of quilt names, black-and-white and color
photos and a bibliography. Examples of quilts: Iris, Poppy, Sunflower and Dogwood. Black-and-white illustration of a fifth-century
appliqué, a modern Egyptian Double Nine-Patch, and Baskets. Some
illustrations of quilting designs: Deamonts Fan, Shell, Rope, Feathers, Medallion. Emphasis on history of quiltmaking going back to
biblical times. Photo of Funeral Tent of an Egyptian Queen. Discusses Antiquity, Middle Ages, Old England and America. General
discussion of collections, exhibitions and quilt names.

243. Weeks, Linda. Patchwork and Other Quilting. New York:
      Sterling Publishing Co. , 1973, 48pp.
         Instructional book for beginners. Sixteen black-and-white
photos, sixteen color photos. Illustrates Grandmothers Flower Garden, Tulip, Lone Star, Bow Tie, Rose, Sunbonnet Sue, Overall

Sam and Baby quilt. Includes metric conversion chart and covers
how to tie and design a quilt. Includes appliqué.

244. _____ and Ippolito, Jo Christensen. Quilting: Patchwork
    and Trapunto. New York: Sterling Publishing Co., Inc., 1980,
    96pp.
            Instructional book. Introductory chapters give overview
of the subject. Patterns for projects such as Bow Tie quilt, Lone
Star and Tulip quilt. Nine in all. Also illustrates projects such
as home accessories, children's clothing, purse and a tote bag. Numerous illustrations, black-and-white and color photos. Includes
index.

245. Weiss, Rita. The How to Candlewick Quilt. Northbrook, Ill.:
    Pattern People, 1982, 18pp.
            Directions with black-and-white illustrations, full-size
patterns and color cover. Twelve designs.

246. _____. Quick 'n Easy Candlewick. Northbrook Ill.: ASN
    Publishing, 1983, 22pp.
            Color cover. Black-and-white photos and illustrations.
Full-size patterns for flowers, alphabet and Sunbonnet Sue. Instructions for small items such as Christmas ornaments.

247. Wilson, Erica. Erica Wilson's Quilts of America. Birming-
    ham, Ala.: Oxmoor House, 1979, 218pp.
            Color photos of quilts from the Great American Quilt Con-
test held in 1977. Includes patterns for sixteen of the winning quilts.
Contains an index, bibliography, list of suppliers for such things as
seamstress pressing, photo sensitizing emulsion and fiber dye companies. Annotation accompanying the photos notes technique (machine
or hand) and directions for assembly and finishing. Examples such
as Ray of Light, Winner's Circle, Seminole Indian quilt and May
Garden. Discusses trapunto, Hawaiian, hexagons, yo-yo, cathedral
window and strip quilts. Shows crazy quilt with stitches and instructions. Discusses the use of crayons, painting, dying and photography.

248. 'Woman's Day' Prize Winning Quilts, Coverlets and Afghans.
    New York: Sedgewood Press, 1982, 255pp.
            Thirty-five winning items from Woman's Day Afghan and
Coverlet contest. Part One is devoted to sewn and embroidered designs including quilts (pp. 9-126). Shows Mariner's Compass, Bear
Paw, Triple Irish Chain and contemporary quilts; eighteen in all.
General directions for quilting (pp. 234-242). Includes color photo
of the finished quilt, noting size, materials needed and directions.
Illustrates both block and quilting patterns, some full-size, others
reduced. Discusses assembling, quilting and finishing. Gives name
of artist, her/his town and state and a short statement on the design
and on the artist. Five pages of illustrated embroidery stitches.

249. Woodard, Thomas K. and Greenstein, Blanche. Crib Quilts
    and Other Small Wonders. New York: E. P. Dutton, 1981,
    136pp.

Extensive essay on childhood clothing, crib quilts and learning to sew. Discusses storing, showing and cleaning crib quilts. Color photos of 163 small Amish quilts, pieced and appliquéd. One page illustrates smaller items. Annotations note description, date, provenance, size and collection. Patterns and instructions (pp. 86-331) for making a crib quilt. Lists suppliers and suggested books. Full-size patterns for thirteen quilts, noting fabric requirements, finished dimensions and directions. Illustrates the quilt and gives piecing diagram for patterns such as Star, Medallion, Baskets and School House.

250.   Wooster, Ann.   Quiltmaking, The Modern Approach to a Traditional Craft. New York: Drake Publishers, 1972, 160pp.
Instructions for patchwork, appliqué and small items such as belts, pillows, glass case, handbag, tie, skirts and aprons. Section on modern quilting. Chapter on patchwork such as Log Cabin, stars, parallelograms, curved seam; appliqué such as florals and reverse appliqué; section on creating a design. Eighteen-item bibliography, forty-eight-word glossary.

II. EXHIBITION CATALOGS

251. Akana, Elizabeth. Hawaiian Quilting: A Fine Art, Including
a catalog of the exhibition, "Hawaiian Quilt Display" held at
the Mission Houses Museum June 9-14, 1981. Lihue, Hawaii:
Kauai Museum, 1981, 48pp.
   Opening statement by Ms. Akana on the history and technique of Hawaiian quilting. She states that it is a combination of
native creativity and the instructions of the first New England mis-
sionaries. Discusses why so few of the old quilts survive and why
similar patterns have different names. Forty-nine black-and-white
photographs of quilts from the show; some detail photos. Information
given on each quilt: Hawaiian name with English meaning, maker's
name, fabric, color, date, style of quilting, size, owner's name,
who it was made for, variant name for pattern. Examples: Pineapple (1935), Tahitian Beauty (n. d.), Hawaiian Garden (1910), Blue
Jade (1976), Pua Pake (c. 1915) and My Beloved Flag (c. 1900).
Also includes some black-and-white illustrations showing piecing,
cutting and sewing for specific patterns.

252. Albacete, M. J.; D'Atri, Sharon and Reeves, Jane. Ohio
Quilts: A Living Tradition. Canton, Ohio: The Canton Art
Institute, 1981, 59pp.
   Documents show held from January 28 through March 14,
1981. Features antique, Amish and contemporary quilts made in
Ohio, dated from 1800 through 1981. M. J. Albacete, Associate
Director of the Gallery, searched for quilts that "showed traditional
concepts as well as examples by modern artists." It includes a
discussion of nineteenth-century quilts followed by thirty-four examples. Color and black-and-white photos are accompanied by a description of the quilt: style, date, size, place of origin, maker,
museum location and a short annotation. Examples: I: Broderie
Perse (1835-46), Linsey-woolsey wholecloth (1820), Turkey Tracks
(1840), floral wreath appliqué (1875); II: Twenty Amish quilts from
the collection of Darwin Bearley in color and black-and-white photos,
e. g., Roman Stripes (1880), Nine Patch (1880), Railroad Crossing
(1914), Broken Dishes (1925); III: Twenty-three contemporary quilts,
e. g., Bittersweet XIV, XV, XIII by Nancy Crow and The Oberlin
Quilt (c. 1974); Black Dhurrie by Marjorie Claybrook; Judi Warren's
Hot Mobius 1980; Wenda von Weise's Kneade Farm; Sunset (1978).
Also includes directions with full-size patterns for making an Ohio
Star quilt.

253. American Crafts Council. Museum of Contemporary Crafts.
The New American Quilt. New York: The Museum, 1976, 20pp.

Exhibition catalog for show held from April 1 through
June 13, 1976, circulated by the Western Association of Art Museums.   Curated by Ruth Amdur Tenenhaus.   Emphasis is on artists
using innovative techniques such as soft sculpture, three dimensions,
tie-dye, silkscreen, batik and photosensitized cloth.   Includes statement by Jonathan Holstein, seven color and thirteen black-and-white
photos.   Also gives dimensions, technique and artist's name.   Examples: Untitled (1974), by Risa Goldman; Hank Williams Bigger
than Life (1974), by Sandra Humberson; The Mountain from My Window (1975), by Helen Bitar; Puzzle of the Floating World No. 3
(1975), by Katherine Westphal.

254.   Artists' Quilts: Quilts by Ten Contemporary Artists in Col-
        laboration with Ludy Strauss.   Published in association with
        Harold I. Huhas, n.p., 1981, 31pp.
                Includes statement by Robert MacDonald, Chief Curator
of the La Jolla Museum of Contemporary Art.   A bibliography on
each artist lists his/her exhibitions.   Also includes a checklist of
the eighteen quilts from the show.   Color and black-and-white photos
of contemporary quilts by artists such as Peter Alexander, Charles
Arnoldi and Tony Berlant.   Show traveled to the La Jolla Museum of
Contemporary Art; the Los Angeles Municipal Art Gallery; the San
Jose Museum of Art and the University Art Gallery of the University
of Texas at Arlington.

255.   Atlanta Historical Society. Southern Comfort: Quilts from the
        Atlanta Historical Society Collection.   Atlanta: Atlanta Histor-
        ical Society, 1978, 50pp.
                Catalog for a show held from June 4 through October 7,
1978 at McElreath Hall.   Eleven-item bibliography; sixteen black-
and-white photos of quilts from the society's collection.   Color cover.
Introduction by Elizabeth Reynolds.   This was an exhibit of seventeen
nineteenth-century pieced and appliquéd quilts selected for their overall condition and visual appeal.   All except three of these quilts are
from the South and most are from Georgia.   Examples: Rolling Pin
Wheel, Star of Bethlehem, Wild Goose Chase, a signature quilt, Barn
Raising, Brides Quilt and Rose of Sharon.   Quilt photos accompanied
by pertinent information.

256.   Beaverbrook Art Gallery, Fredericton, New Brunswick, Canada.
        Quilts by Teruko Inoue.   Fredericton, N. B.: The Gallery,
        1978, 3pp.
                This checklist catalog documents an exhibition of twenty-
five quilts.   Black-and-white cover photo of the artist's quilt, Pineapple, cat. no. 6.   Introduction written by Ian Lumsden, gallery
curator.   Examples of quilts: Labyrinth, Pandora's Box, Star of
Bethlehem, 100 Pyramids and Steps to Heaven.

257.   Betterton, Sheila. The American Quilt Tradition. Bath, Eng-
        land: The American Museum in Britain, 1976, 57pp.
                Documents a show at the Commonwealth Art Gallery in
London held from July 23 through September 2, 1976.   Gives a brief
history of quilting as it traveled from Europe to the United States.

Compares and contrasts American quilts at the American Museum
in Britain with British examples from the eighteenth through the
twentieth centuries.   Gives annotated examples.   Bibliography.

258. _____ . Quilts and Coverlets From the American Museum
      in Britain. Bath, England: The American Museum in Britain,
      1978, 128pp.
            Categorizes the museum collection as: plain quilts,
pieced, appliqué, crazy, candlewick, woven, stencilled, embroidered
and trapunto. One hundred color photos, six black-and-white photos,
color cover, index and twenty-three-item bibliography. Each category introduced by an essay. Photos annotated with descriptive paragraph and factual data such as provenance, date, size, name and
donor's name. Some examples: Blue whole-cloth quilt (eighteenth
century), Orange Baskets quilt (nineteenth century), Princess Feather
(nineteenth century), Mary Young's coverlet (candlewick, 1821), woven
coverlet (early nineteenth century), coverlet (stencilled, 1830) and
embroidered top (late nineteenth century).

259. Bevier Gallery. College of Fine and Applied Arts. Rochester
      Institute of Technology. Art Americana: Quilts and Coverlets.
      Rochester, N. Y.: Rochester Institute of Technology, 1975,
      25pp.
            Twenty color plates of eighteen quilts and two woven cover-
lets from private collections, the Rochester Musuem and Science
Center and the Holstein/Van Der Hoof collection. Most of the quilts
are geometric patterns. Description of plates notes pattern name,
quilt size, date, collection and fabric. Some examples: Ribbon
Stripe (1940), Log Cabin, Birds in the Air, Village Scene (c. 1947),
Baby Block and Rainbow quilt top (c. 1940). Color cover: Roman
Bar (c. 1920).

260. Bits of Fabric and Scraps of Time. Privately printed, 1983,
      10pp.
            Checklist of quilts and photographs exhibited at the Na-
tional Humanities Center in Raleigh, North Carolina from February
19 to 20 and 26 to 27, 1983. Sponsored by the Capital Quilters
Guild and the Durham-Orange Quilters. Part I: twenty-six quilts
and photographs; Part II: seventy-nine contemporary quilts. Checklist notes name of quilt, maker's name and a brief description.

261. Black Belt to Hill Country: Alabama Quilts from the Robert
      and Helen Cargo Collection. Birmingham, Ala.:   Birmingham
      Museum of Art, 1981, 92pp.
            Documents show at the Birmingham Museum of Art held
from December 13, 1981 through January 24, 1982, and at the Mont-
gomery Museum of Art from September 16 through November 14,
1982. Sixty black-and-white photos; eleven color photos; bibliography
and color cover. The Cargo collection of almost 300 quilts represents "most types of quilts and quilting techniques done in the South."
Most examples are from the nineteenth century; some are from the
1930's through the 1950's. Introduction by Robert T. Cargo discusses
the collection and specific examples in the catalog. Includes essays

"In the Words of Women: Daily Lives of Southern Women," with footnotes, by Gail C. Andrews, the museum's curator of decorative arts, and "Quilt Women," with footnotes, by Janet Strain McDonald, assistant curator of decorative arts. Also contains a 1981 interview with quilters. Each photo accompanied by the quilt name, date, maker's name, county, size and brief description. Examples: Tree of Life (c. 1875-80), Snail Trails (1875-80), Crescents (c. 1870), album quilt (c. 1872), Whig Rose (c. 1820), Morning Glory (c. 1930-35) and Mystery Circle (c. 1960).

262. Bordes, Marilynn Johnson. 12 Great Quilts From the Ameri-
      can Wing. New York: The Metropolitan Museum of Art, 1974,
      36pp.
            Exhibition catalog for a show held from May 7 through
September 3, 1974 at the museum. The pieced and appliquéd quilts
in the show date from 1800 through 1920. They illustrate a design
tradition rather than an overview of the art. The examples are
arranged in chronological order according to style and technique and
portray the evolution of manufactured printed and dyed fabric. Includes a bibliography.

263. Bowes Museum. Barnard's Castle, Durham, England. North
      Country Quilting. Hounslow, England: The Museum, 1963,
      20pp.
            Miss Anne Ward curated this show of forty quilts and re-
lated items held from July 12 to October 1, 1963. Catalog contains
an introductory essay entitled "North Country Quilting." Annotations
give a brief description, the owner's name, quilt size and date.
Items are divided by locale: Cumberland, Yorkshire, etc. Five detail photos. Now out of print.

264. Brevard Art Center and Museum. Deanna Powell: Solo Ex-
      hibition of Quilts. Melbourne, Fla.: Brevard Art Center,
      1983, 11pp.
            Exhibition catalog for show held from July 3 through
August 7, 1983. Color cover: Indira quilt. Foreword by Robert
Gabriel, director of the musuem; introduction by Pat Kyser, con-
tributing editor for Quilt World Magazine. Also includes statement
by the artist, her resumé and checklist of eleven quilts in the show
dating from 1971 to 1983. Black-and-white photos of Quiltability
(1980), Four Seasons Series: Winter Stars (1981), 'Dee' Lightful
Ribbons (1981) and Four Seasons Series: Summer Shells (1982).

265. Brooks, Marylin. World of Quilts at Meadow Brook Hall: A
      Celebration of Matilda Dodge Wilson's 100th Birthday, Rochester,
      Michigan: Oakland University, 1983, 60pp.
            Catalog for show held from September 8 to 25, 1983 at
Meadow Brook Hall. Introductory statement by Robert Bishop.
Twenty-two black-and-white photos; 109 color photos; color covers.
Lists lenders to the exhibition. Examples of quilts: Schoolhouse
(1981), Stenciled quilt (1830), Tree of Life (1830), Two Amish crib
quilts (c. 1910), Nine-Patch (c. 1875), Celebrity quilt (1981), Sioux
Indian Sampler (1933), Trail of Tears (1979) and George Washington

at Valley Forge (1976). Each photo accompanied by notation on
style, quilt name, date, size, maker's name and any known history.

266. Brunnier Gallery & Museum. Iowa State University. Heir-
      loom to Heirloom: Historic Quilts, Traditional Quilts, Con-
      temporary Quilts. Ames, Iowa: Brunnier Gallery, 1983, 25pp.
            Documents Heirloom to Heirloom Quilt Conference '83
held from July 6 to 9, 1983. Items in the exhibit illustrate trends
in fabric, design and technique. Black-and-white photos of some
of the sixty-three historic quilts noting date, description, size and
owner's name. Examples: Chintz quilt (1731), Mosaic (early 1880's)
and LeMoyne Star (c. 1840-50). The show also included thirty-three
traditional quilts made in Iowa in the last ten years. E. g., Variable Star (1980-81) and Windflower (1982). Contemporary quilt artists such as Helen Bitar, Rhoda Cohn, Nancy Crow, Carol Gribble,
Nancy Halpern, Jean Hewes, Michael James and Judy Matheison also
exhibited.

267. Burke, Mary. Sunshine and Shadows: A Look at Island Quilts
      and Quilting. Charlottetown, Prince Edward Island: Confeder-
      ation Centre Art Gallery and Museum, 1978, 13pp.
            Exhibition catalog for show held from November 23 to
December 31, 1978 at the gallery. It is a "survey of quilting" of the
Islanders. On exhibit were 100 heirloom and contemporary quilts
(pieced, appliquéd and embroidered), as well as other quilted objects
(clothing and wall hangings). The older objects date back to the
1850's; the modern ones are from the twentieth century. The gallery
purchased several items from the show for its permanent collection.
There are fifteen black-and-white photos of quilts in addition to two
black-and-white cover photos. Includes information such as the name
of the design, date of creation, maker's name and where it is housed.
Also lists names of Island quilters exhibiting in the show and con-
tributing collectors and institutions.

268. Burnham, Dorothy K. Pieced Quilts of Ontario. Toronto:
      Royal Ontario Museum, 1975, 64pp.
            Catalog illustrates twenty-seven examples of pieced quilts
made in Ontario, dating from the nineteenth century. Primarily
black-and-white photos (two color) of pieces in the Royal Ontario
Museum's collection. Some quilts are shown in a detail photo.
Photos are accompanied by description, history and construction
diagrams. Examples: Nine-Patch, Irish Chain, Log Cabin and
8, 000 Triangles. At this writing, no further catalogs have been
published.

269. Carlisle, Lilian B. Pieced Work and Appliqué Quilts at Shel-
      burne Museum. (Museum pamphlet series no. 2) Shelburne,
      Vt.: The Museum, 1957, 96pp.
            These quilts are categorized as pieced, pieced and appli-
qué, appliqué, cut-out chintz, album and unclassified designs. Every page contains black-and-white photos from the museum's collection. Each photo accompanied by extensive description. Examples:

Zig-Zag, Civil War counterpane, Lotus Flower, Ann Robinson
spread, Elk and Fawn and Abraham Lincoln spread.   Thirty-three-
item bibliography.   Some detail photos.

270.   Center for the History of American Needlework.   Something
       Old and Something New.   Ambridge, Pa.:   The Center, 1981,
       15pp.
       Catalog documents an exhibition of sixteen modern and
eighteen antiwue quilts and coverlets held in 1981.   Six black-and-
white photos.   E.g., Amish Echoes, Jungle Gym quilt (detail), Scan-
dinavian Peasant quilt (detail), Sampler quilt (detail), Thistle quilt,
Triangles quilt.   Catalog includes full-size pattern for West Mifflin
Flower and Triangles quilt.   Also includes fourteen black-and-white
illustrations of quilt blocks from the 1899 Ladies Art Company Catalog.   The eighteen antique quilts were loaned from private collectors
and museums for the show.   Notation gives name of quilt and brief
information.

271.   Clar, Ricky.   Quilts and Carousels: Folk Art in the Fire-
       lands.   Oberlin, Ohio: Press of the Times, 1983, 52pp.
       The show coincided with the sesquicentennial of Oberlin,
Ohio and the 175th anniversary of the settlement of the Firelands.
It was held from May 1 through July 4, 1983 at the Firelands Association for the Visual Arts.   Seven color, and twenty-one black-and-
white quilt photos.   Text on "Women's Local History in the Firelands and Oberlin" and "Quilters and Carvers: Tradition and Inno-
vation."   Photos accompanied by notation on style, maker's name,
locale, date, size and lender's name.   Examples: appliquéd and
stuffed (1844), appliquéd quilt (1875) and pieced quilt (1979).   Text
documented with footnotes.

272.   Curtis, Phillip. H.   American Quilts in the Newark Museum
       Collection.   Newark, N. J.:   The Newark Museum Assn.,
       1973, 68pp.
       Catalog is volume 25 #3/4 (Summer/Fall 1973) of the
Museum n.s.   It is an inventory of the museum's collection of 120
American quilts dating from the eighteenth century to the present.
Author relates how the collection began and what criteria was employed in choosing representative items.   Catalog illustrates four
categories: pieced, appliqué, combination and all-white.   Each section has photos and descriptions followed by a listing of other quilts
in the same category.   Some of the quilts shown: Delectable Mountains (1840-60), Masonic quilt (c. 1853), Bleeding Heart (1825),
crazy quilt (1885) and All-White Voorhees quilt (1830-31).   Extensive
bibliography.

273.   D. A. R. Museum.   Washington, D. C.   American Quilts:
       1780-1880.   San Francisco: The Art Museum Assn., 1982,
       12pp.
       Exhibition catalog of twenty-five quilts from the D. A. R.
Museum.   Six black-and-white photos: all-over quilting pattern (late
nineteenth century), detail of stuffed white-work (c. 1840), Feather

Star (1840-50), Reverse appliqué (c. 1815), detail of appliqué (c. 1850)
and detail of a crazy quilt (c. 1870). Notations for each of the
twenty-five quilts gives description, maker's name and place, approximate date, size and who bequeathed the gift to the museum. The
catalog illustrates one-piece quilts, white-work, pieced, appliqué
and crazy.

274.   Davison, Mildred.   American Quilts from the Art Institute of
       Chicago.   Chicago: The Art Institute of Chicago, 1966, 40pp.
               Description of forty quilts in the museum's collection.
Includes a bibliography and black-and-white photos of Cherry Wreaths
(1865), Gold Finches and Flowers (1948), Star of Bethlehem (1830),
Wandering Foot (c. 1830), Modern Star (1850), Rose of Sharon (c.
1850) and an all-white quilt from New England dated 1819. A short
description accompanies each quilt photo.

275.   DeGraw, Imelda.   Quilts and Coverlets.   Denver: The Denver
       Art Museum, 1974, 144pp.
               This is a second museum catalog showing 200 works from
the collection.   It documents a show held from June 29 through October 6, 1974.   Includes a bibliography.   Gives the history of pieced,
crazy, appliquéd and woven coverlets.   Most examples are American,
accompanied by notes on the pattern, fabric and locale.   Eight color
photos and 136 black-and-white illustrations.

276.   Dunham, Lydia Roberts.   Quilt Collection.   Denver: The Mu-
       seum, 1963, 124pp.
               This catalog is a 1963 issue of the Denver Art Museum
Quarterly, now out of print (OP).   Primarily black-and-white photos
of quilts in the collection with accompanying detail photo.   Examples
of Double X, Peony, Brides quilt and Rose Tree.   Photos are accompanied by a descriptive paragraph noting the quilt's date and size.
Color cover and bibliography.

277.   Fox, Sandi.   Quilts in Utah: A Reflection of the Western Ex-
       perience.   Salt Lake City, Utah: The Salt Lake Art Center,
       1981, 48pp.
               Documents the show of twenty quilts held from August
14 through October 4, 1981 at the Salt Lake Art Center.   Essay on
the migration of pioneer women to Utah and the quilts they brought
with them or made along the way.   Examples of quilts: Rose of
Sharon (c. 1820), Ark and Doves (c. 1865), Barn Raising (c. 1860),
Whig Rose (c. 1875) and In God We Trust (1894).   Catalog lists the
quilt name, maker's name, place of origin, date, fabric, size,
lender's name, history and description, including family history.
Twenty-four color photos, some detail photos, color cover, seventeen-
item bibliography.

278.   _____.   Small Endearments: Nineteenth Century Quilts for
       Children and Dolls.   Los Angeles, Calif.:   Los Angeles Muni-
       cipal Art Gallery Associates, 1980, 70pp.

Published for the exhibition of the same name held at the
museum from December 9, 1980 through January 15, 1981. Black-
and-white and color photos of many of the 193 quilts in the show.
Examples and discussion of whole cloth, pieced, all-white, Broderie
Perse, pieced and appliqué combination, appliqué and pressed. Includes examples of Pennsylvania Dutch and Amish. Catalog lists
the quilt name, place of origin, size, date of construction and present owner. Essay on childhood and parents' relationships to their
children. Discusses each kind of quilt and refers to specific examples in the catalog.

279.   Freeman, June.   Quilting Patchwork and Appliqué, 1700-1982:
        Sewing as a Woman's Art. London: The Minories, 1983, 24pp.
                 Documents the Minories Touring Exhibition held at the
Crafts Council Gallery, London, from February 16 through April 3,
1983.   Introduction by Jeremy Theophilus, Curator at The Minories.
Ten-page essay on the importance of quilting, accompanied by footnotes.   Thirteen color and five black-and-white quilt photos.   Three
photos showing social circumstances of the quiltmakers.   Catalog of
eighty-three items divided into Early British work, North Country
work, Welsh work, American work and contemporary work.   Catalog lists artist's name, date and size of quilt, with description and
an eighteen-item glossary.

280.   Freeman, Roland L.   Something to Keep You Warm: The
        Roland Freeman Collection of Black American Quilts from the
        Mississippi Heartland. Jackson, Miss.: Mississippi Dept. of
        Archives and History, 1981, 46pp.
                 Preface by Patti Carr Black, director, Mississippi State
Historical Museum. Two-page essay on "Slave Quilting on Ante-
Bellum Plantations," by Gladys-Marie Fry. Three-page essay on
"The Aesthetics of Afro-American Quilts," by Maude Southwell
Wahlman, accompanied by footnotes. Introduction by Roland L.
Freeman, curator. This was an exhibition at the State History Mu-
seum in the summer of 1981, of twenty-five quilts from a collection
of over fifty. Color photos of all the quilts, accompanied by a black-
and-white photo of the artist, with her name, birthdate, county, quilt
name, year made and size. Statement about the quilter accompanies
each photo. The majority of the quilts date from the 1960's through
the 1980's; some from the 1930's and 1940's. Examples: Five
Colored Girls (1980), Slave Chain (1969), Trees at Sunset (1972),
Rainbow Blocks (1975), Windmill Blades (1935-40) and Diamond in
a Square (1949). Most are pieced, some appliquéd.

281.   Frye, L. Thomas, ed.   American Quilts, A Handmade Legacy.
        Oakland, Calif.: The Oakland Museum, 1981, 86pp.
                 Exhibition of nineteenth- and twentieth-century quilts held
from December 14, 1980 through February 22, 1981 at the Oakland
Museum.   The quilts are viewed as objects used through birth, child-
hood, marriage, family and death.   Essays by Inez Brooks-Myers,
Pat Ferrero, Linda Reuther, Julie Silber, Elaine Hedges, Debra
Heimerdinger and Stephanie Krebs.   Color and black-and-white photos.
Catalog now out of print.

282. Garvan, Beatrice B. <u>The Pennsylvania German Collection.</u>
Philadelphia: The Philadelphia Museum of Art, 1982, 372 pp.
      This book documents the entire Pennsylvania German art-
ifacts collection of the museum. The author has devoted pp. 263-
265 to quilts. Black-and-white photos of ten quilts, dating from
1840 to 1900, with date, description and size. Does not give specific name of each quilt. Notation lists fabric, design, construction
and quilting pattern.

283. Gilman, Carolyn and Westbrook, Nicholas. <u>Minnesota Patch-
      work.</u> St. Paul, Minn.: Minnesota Historical Society, 1979, 9pp.
      Describes thirty-five quilts from the Minnesota Historical
Society show held in 1979. Cover photo. Gives name of pattern,
date, size and history of each quilt. Examples: Blazing Sun (1850's),
Hovering Hawk variation (late 1800's), Double Irish Chain (1850's),
Lady of the Lake variation (c. 1900) and Baby Block (c. 1900).
Quilts are from the society's collection.

284. Gish, Enola M. <u>Kansas Quilt Treasurers II: An Exhibition
      of Twenty Kansas Quilts 100 Years Old and Older.</u> Logan,
      Kan.: The Dane G. Hansen Memorial Museum Assoc., Inc.,
      1983, 20pp.
      Thirteen black-and-white photos and seven color photos
accompanied by historical information on the family who owned it,
the quilt itself and current owner. Some photos of the quiltmakers
or owners. Examples of both pieced and appliqué quilts: Broken
Star (1850), Feathered Square (1880), Masterpiece of Roses (1845),
Flags and Eagles (1880) and Star Medallion (1860).

285. Gross, Joyce. <u>A Galaxy of Quilts.</u> Privately printed, 1983,
      16pp.
      Checklist of seventy-five quilts shown at the West Coast
Quilters Conference VI from July 19 through 22, 1983. They date
from 1830 to 1983. Annotated with pattern name, owner, maker,
date, size and brief description. Examples: Melon Patch (1920),
Whitework (1830), Roman Stripe (1900) and Amish Log Cabin (1978).

286. _____. <u>A Patch in Time: A Catalog of Antique, Traditional
      and Contemporary Quilts.</u> Mill Valley, Calif.: The Mill Valley
      Quilt Authority, 1973, 32pp.
      Catalog of sixty-eight antique and modern quilts. Twenty-
five quilts illustrated in full, and detail black-and-white photos.
Color cover: The Hardman Quilt. Notation gives pertinent information accompanied by a paragraph describing the quilt and its history. E.g., Matterhorn (1934); Our Pride (1945), by Charlotte J.
Whitehall; Falling Leaves (1973); trapunto Fruit Basket (1845); Cal-
endula and Paradise Garden (1945), both by Rose Kretsinger; Myths,
by Betty DeMars (1965) and Cigarband Quilt (c. 1900).

287. _____. <u>Patch in Time #4.</u> Privately printed, 1979, 22pp.
      Checklist of seventy quilts shown at the Jack Tar Hotel
in San Francisco from June 30 through July 3, 1979. Gives the
quilt name, size, maker, provenance, date, owner and brief description. Also lists names and addresses of thirty-six exhibitors.

288. _____. Quilts of the West. San Francisco: Bank of America World Headquarters, 1976, 14pp.
        Essay by the author on the growing importance of quilt-
making in pioneer life as evidenced by book publication and quilt
shows. This catalog documents a show held at the Bank of America
World Headquarters from February 16 through March 26, 1976.
Twenty-eight quilts dating from 1832 to 1975. Examples: Matterhorn, from the Denver Art Museum; Paradise Garden, by Charlotte
Whitehall from the University of Kansas Museum of Art and Wreath
of Roses, by Rose Kretsinger. Each quilt annotated with name of
maker, owner, size and what book it is pictured in, if any. Descriptive paragraph on each. No photos. Color cover.

289. Hagerman, Betty J. and Ericson, Helen M., eds. Kansas
        Quilt Symposium 1978. Baldwin City, Kan.: Kaw Valley Quilt-
ers Guild, 1979, 80pp.
        Documents that portion of the show held at the Student
Union and the Kansas Symposium show. There are also some photos
of contemporary quilts that were shown at the Lawrence Art Center
Thirty-four color photos of quilts, either full or detail. Over 100
photographs in black-and-white. Photos accompanied by quilt name,
description and date, owner's name and maker's name. Includes
Chris W. Edmonds' George Washington at Valley Forge, and The
Spooners quilts; A Kansas Pattern, by Charlotte J. Whitehall and A
Meeting of the Sunbonnet Children, by Betty Hagerman.

290. Helen Foresman Spencer Museum of Art. University of Kansas.
        150 Years of American Quilts. Lawrence, Kan.: The Museum,
1973, 56pp.
        This is a catalog of the museum's collection of pieced,
appliquéd, stuffed and combination quilts. Contains an index, bibliography and fifty illustrations. It includes the William B. Thayer
Memorial, the Kretsinger collection and the Malcom-James collection.
The description gives the date, material and size of the quilt. Examples: Bandanna With Four Patch, Job's Troubles, Chips and Whetstones, Moss Ross and Tulip Tree.

291. _____. Quilters Choice: Quilts from the Museum Collection. Lawrence, Kan.: The Museum, 1978, 80pp.
        Written in cooperation with the Kaw Valley Quilters Guild.
Eight color and seventy black-and-white photos. Now out of print.

292. Holstein, Jonathan. Abstract Design in American Quilts. New
        York: The Whitney Museum of American Art, 1971, 16pp.
        Catalog for the exhibit at the Whitney in 1971 showing
quilts in geometric patterns. Six photos and a cover photo.

293. _____. American Pieced Quilts. New York: Viking Press,
1972, 94pp.
        Portrays quilts selected for their "painterly" quality.
Gives a short history of the craft, with twenty-one color and sixty-
four black-and-white photos and a thirty-item bibliography. Examples of quilts: Basket of Scraps (1860), Cup & Saucer (1910), Rain-

bow (1880), Sawtooth (1875) and Tree Everlasting (1850).   Notation
gives place of origin, approximate date, fabric and size.   Circulated
by the Smithsonian Institution's Traveling Exhibition Service.   Traveled to the Musée des Arts Decoratifs and the Stedelejk Museum.

294.   _____, and Finley, John.   Kentucky Quilts 1800-1900:   The
       Kentucky Quilt Project.   Louisville, Ky.:   The Kentucky Quilt
       Project, 1982, 79pp.
            Quilt commentaries by Jonathan Holstein, historical text
by John Finley.   Holstein discusses quilting as an American art and
craft.   Finley discusses the evolution of the Kentucky Quilt Project.
Catalog contains color photos accompanied by photos of the quiltmaker; annotations give pertinent information on the quilt.   Photos
are interspersed by text on Kentucky and the family history of the
quiltmakers.   Sixty-two color plates of quilts, some detail photos.
Seven-item bibliography on Kentucky.   Examples: Log Cabin (1885),
Bear's Paw (c. 1865), North Carolina Lily (1865), New York
Beauty (c. 1875) and Star (1876).   Contains list of lenders.

295.   _____ ;   _____ and van der Hoof, Gail.   Quilts Paris:
       Musée des Arts Decoratifs.   Paris: Edition des Massons,
       1972, 96pp.
            Documents the show of nineteenth-century American quilts.
Eighty-three illustrations and a bibliography.   Discusses history of
quilting from Colonial days through the nineteenth century.

296.   Hunter Museum of Art.   A Patchwork Garden.   Chattanooga,
       Tenn.:   The Museum, 1981, 36pp.
            The quilt show was part of the Southern Quilt Symposium
and was held at the Hunter from April 7 through May 30, 1981.   The
exhibit featured antique and contemporary examples of floral quilts.
Thirty-nine full and some detail black-and-white photos.   The forty-
eight quilts in the show date from 1830 to 1890, and 1950 to 1981.
E. g., Tulips at Midnight (1981), Garland of Flowers (1963) and Appalachian Daisy (1900).
            Examples also include the Last Rose of Summer (stuffed
construction), by Sidney H. Weeter and the Blooming Jacket, by
Diana Suarey (clothing).   Hazel Carter, Flanin Glover, Bets Ramsey,
Nancy Crow, Georgia Bonesteel and Marjorie Puckett exhibited in
the show.

297.   _____.   Quilt Close-up: Five Southern Views, A Study of
       of Regionalism in Quiltmaking.   Chattanooga, Tenn.:   1983,
       46pp.
            Twenty-four quilts exhibited at the Hunter from March 6
through May 1, 1983.   Ten black-and-white and fourteen color photographs.   Examples of quilts from Macon County, North Carolina
(nineteenth century); East Tennessee; Redbud, Georgia (1873-1907);
Sand Mountain, Alabama and modern quilts from the Mississippi
Heartland.
            Includes a discussion of each region, noting the quilters,
the times in which they lived and the quilt fabric.   Photos of such

quilts as Cotton Boll (c. 1855), Sixteen-Patch (1830), Wheel of Fortune (1890), North Carolina Lily (1881) and Log Cabin strip quilt
(1950).

298. Illinois State University, Normal. Center for the Visual Arts.
      200 Years of American Quilts in Illinois Private Collections.
      Norman: The University, 1976, 46pp.
            Historical introduction by Bonnie Belshe; Juror's com-
      ments by Patsy and Myron Orlofsky. A traveling exhibit of fifty-
      seven antique and contemporary quilts never before displayed publicly.
      Forty-five black-and-white photos including one detail; thirteen color
      photos. Catalog notes quilt name, date, size, history, description
      and lender's name. E. g., Star of the Bluegrass (1971), Log Cabin
      (c. 1830), Flying Geese (1920), Sunbeam (1930-40), Barn Raising
      (1888), Broken Star (1894), Triple Irish Chain (1925) and Sherlock
      Holmes quilt (contemporary).

299. International Exhibitions Foundation. American Quiltmakers.
      Washington, D. C.: The Foundation, n. d., brochure.
            One-page brochure with statement and checklist of twenty
      quilts made from 1973 through 1975. Organized in cooperation with
      the DeCordova Museum, Lincoln, Massachusetts.

300. _____. American Textiles. Washington, D. C.: The Foun-
      dation, n. d., 4pp.
            Items loaned by the National Gallery of Art from the In-
      dex of American Design. Fifty-item checklist includes three quilts.

301. _____. Morning Star Quilts: Art of the Plains Indians.
      Washington, D. C.: The Foundation, n. d., 2pp.
            Brochure checklist of the twenty quilts in the exhibit with
      a one-page curator's statement. Checklist gives name of artist,
      title and quilt size. All are from the collection of Florence Pulford,
      Los Altos, California.

302. Irish Bedcovers: Techniques and Traditions. Holywood, Ul-
      ster: The Ulster Folk and Transport Museum, 1981, 6pp.
            Checklist of bedcovers shown from the Fall 1981 through
      Spring 1982, mounted by the Ulster Folk and Transport Museum, The
      National Museum of Ireland and Muckross House, Killarney. Forty
      items are divided into four groups: quilting (1827-1981), patchwork
      (late eighteenth century through 1980), embroidery (eighteenth cen-
      tury through 1915) and knitting/crochet (1887 through the 1920's).

303. Janos, Barbara S. Amish Quilts (1870-1930) A Graphic State-
      ment from a Plain People. Privately printed. Out of print,
      5pp.
            Documents the collection of Barbara S. Janos and Bar-
      bara Ross. Twenty quilts annotated with pattern name, type, place
      of origin, date, size and description. Nine black-and-white photos.

304. Johnson, Bruce. A Child's Comfort: Baby and Doll Quilts in
      American Folk Art. New York: Harcourt Brace Jovanovich,
      1977, 116pp.

Written in collaboration with Susan S. Connor, Josephine
Rogers and Holly Sidford, in association with the Museum of American Folk Art. Catalog for the show at the museum held from October 5, 1976 through January 23, 1977. Eighteen-item glossary,
footnotes and an eleven-item bibliography. Essay on childhood in
the nineteenth century. Color and black-and-white quilt photos with
illustrations and pertinent information. Chapter on making a child's
quilt, by Josephine Rogers, including directions, patterns and color
guide. Chapter on caring for and displaying quilts. Examples of
quilts shown: Pinwheel (1890), Chintz cutout (1863), Star of Bethlehem (1930) and Baby's Blocks (1860).

305. Johnson, Theta; Christensen, Jean; Snow, Phyllis and Smith,
     Jay. Antique Quilts of Utah. Logan, Utah: Cooperative Ex-
     tension Service, Utah State University, 1977, 59pp.
          Accompanies a slide show of quilts shown at the 1977
Festival of the American West at Utah State University. Each quilt
is documented as seventy-five years old or older. Some quilts illustrate the art and heritage of their era. Fifty-six black-and-white
photos with annotations. Examples: Sunburst, Lone Star, Crazy
Patch, Barn Raising, Georgetown Circles, New York Beauty and
Nine-Patch.

306. Jones, Stella M. Hawaiian Quilts. Honolulu, Hawaii: Hono-
     lulu Academy of Arts, 1930, 53pp. Out of print.
          Black-and-white photos with footnotes. Examples: Bird
of Paradise, Pearl of the Pacific, Carrier Pigeon and Ohelo Berries.

307. _____. Hawaiian Quilts. 2nd ed. Honolulu, Hawaii: Hono-
     lulu Academy of Arts, 1973, 78pp.
          Published in cooperation with the Daughters of Hawaii,
the Honolulu Academy of Arts and the Mission Houses Museum exhibition. Originally published at the time of the 1930 exhibition.
The second edition contains small black-and-white photos of quilts
from that show, a section on quilt designs, pattern descriptions and
a discussion of the ethics of pattern duplication.
          The second edition is a catalog for the show entitled The
Quilt--A Hawaiian Heritage held at the Honolulu Academy of Arts
from October 13 through November 18, 1973. It is considered a
permanent file on quilts made prior to 1940. Black-and-white and
color photos. Examples: Prickly Pear, Crown of India, Breadfruit
and Press Gently. Notations relate where the quilt can be found,
and give its size and date.

308. Katzenberg, Dena S. Baltimore Album Quilts. Baltimore:
     Baltimore Museum of Art, 1981, 124pp.
          Documents quilts made in Baltimore between 1846 and
1852. Includes essays on quiltmakers, fabrics and stitching. Relates the Baltimore Album quilt to the social and cultural history of
the city. Contains chapters on pattern design and the City of Baltimore including architecture, the Methodist religion, and the needle-
women such as Mary Evans and Achsah Wilkins. The catalog lists
twenty-four quilts in the exhibit, noting their date, who they were

made for, the collection they are from, the number of squares, size, technique, description of sashing and border and a detailed description of the quilts and their family history. Eleven of the twenty-four plates in the catalog are in color. Author describes block inscriptions and autographs. Extensive bibliography.

The show also traveled to the Museum of Fine Arts in Houston and the Metropolitan Museum of Art in New York City.

309. _____. The Great American Coverup: Counterpanes of the Eighteenth and Nineteenth Centuries. Baltimore: Baltimore Museum of Art, 1971, 48pp.

Black-and-white examples of woven work, trapunto, pieced, embroidered and appliqué quilts. Examples: Pinwheel (1840), Sun Flower (1840), Double Irish Chain (1856), Block and Star (1830) and Ohio Star (1800). Includes bibliography.

310. Kingston Ontario, Queens University. Agnes Etherington Art Centre. Tradition Plus One: Patchwork Quilts from South Eastern Ontario. Kingston: The University, n.d., 16pp.

Exhibit circulated from July 1974 through June 1976. Color and black-and-white photos of thirty-two contemporary works. Traditional patterns such as Maple Leaf, Bow Tie, Railroad, Court House Steps and Grandmother's Fan illustrate both geometric designs and appliqué. Catalog lists the artists and group quilters, with a note on care of quilts and a list of suppliers of quilt patterns in Montreal. Kim Ondaatje curated the entire show.

311. Labe, Beverly and Barber, Frances. American Quilts/European and American Samplers. Glens Falls, N. Y., 1974, 6pp.

This is a checklist of twenty-one quilts exhibited from October 12 through November 9, 1974 at the Hyde Collection Gallery in Glens Falls, New York. Mrs. Beverly Labe, of Adirondack Memories in Glens Falls, authored the quilt section of the catalog. The quilts date from the eighteenth to the early twentieth centuries. Catalog contains one black-and-white detail photo of a trapunto bride's quilt (c. 1800). Cover photo of American Shields (1844). The catalog notes the pattern name, date, size, owner's name, and briefly describes each quilt. E. g., Pieced linsey-woolsey (c. 1780) from Pennsylvania and Flower Garden Album (c. 1840) from the collection of Florence Peto, with five others from her collection. Also contains a short statement about Florence Peto on the last page of the catalog.

312. Louisville Art Gallery. Louisville Quilts. Louisville, Ky.: Louisville Art Gallery, 1980, 4pp.

Brochure documenting exhibit held from November 1980 through January 1981. Contains introduction by Roberta Williams, a coordinator's statement by Katy Christopherson, a color photo of the quilt Louisville Landmarks-1980 and a checklist of forty-seven quilts made by groups in Louisville.

313. Manchester Historical Society. A Sea Side Quilting Bee.
      Manchester-By-The-Sea, Mass.: The Society, 1983, 10pp.
            Mimeographed catalog of show held at the society during
      the summer of 1983. Lists fifty-three antique quilts with descrip-
      tion, date, maker's name and lender's name. No photos. Some
      quilts are from the society's collection. Examples: Log Cabin silk
      quilt (c. 1885), unfinished Baby Block crib quilt, Victorian crazy
      (1886), Sunbonnet Sue (c. 1930), Ohio Star (nineteenth century) and
      Lone Star (1910-30) from Texas.

314. Meldum, Alex. Irish Patchwork. Kilkenny, Republic of Ire-
      land: Kilkenny Design Workshops Ltd., 1979, 66p.
            Catalog of forty-eight quilts from both Northern Ireland
      and the Republic of Ireland. Introduction by Mrs. Laura Jones, then
      assistant keeper of textiles at the Ulster Folk and Transport Museum.
      Fifty-nine color photos of quilts, some detail photos. The quilts
      are categorized by type: Log Cabin, mosaic (various examples of
      pieced work) and mosaic and appliqué. No individual names are
      given to the quilts. Each picture is accompanied by a short descrip-
      tion, including county of origin, size, date and owner's name.

315. Melvin, Patricia Mooney. Ohio Quilts and Quilters 1800-1981.
      Wooster, Ohio: Office of Publications, The College of Wooster
      and the Collier Printing Co., 1981, 58pp.
            Documents a 1981 exhibition/symposium. Contains a two-
      page bibliography of books and articles; eighteen black-and-white quilt
      photos with a description noting date, size, place of origin and owner;
      a short biography of the quilter and the history of the quilt. Text
      documented with footnotes. Also lists lecturers and their topics.
      Introduction by Mary B. Breckenridge; essay "Quilts As Social Docu-
      ments: Forms and Functions of Women's Handiwork," by Mrs.
      Mooney.

316. Michael James: Quiltmaker. Fabric Constructions: The Art
      Quilt. Worcester, Mass.: The Worcester Craft Center, 1983,
      21pp.
            Documents a joint exhibition of a retrospective show of
      Michael James' work and the work of ten other quilt artists. Six-
      teen black-and-white photos; four color photos. Includes biography/
      resumé of each artist; essays by Nancy Halpern, David Hornung and
      Michael James. Examples of James' work: La Tempete, Spring
      Rain, Meadow Lily, Night Sky I (Detail) and City Rhythms. Other
      artists exhibiting: Radka Donnell, Patsy Allen, Pauline Burbidge,
      Rhoda Cohen, Nancy Halpern, Jean Hewes, David Hornung, Terrie
      Hancock Mangat, Jan Myers and Pamela Studstill. Photos of their
      work accompanied by biographies.

317. Mill Valley Quilt Authority. Patch in Time. Privately printed,
      1972, 4pp.

Checklist of fifty-seven modern and antique quilts, and
fifteen smaller items exhibited from October 14 through 15, 1972
at Mill Valley, California.   Notes quilt name, fabric, maker, provenance and owner.

318. _____. A Patch in Time #3.   Privately printed, 1976,
      19pp.
            Checklist of sixty-three antique and contemporary quilts
in the exhibit held from April 2 through 4, 1976 in Mill Valley, California.   Lists pattern name, owner, size, maker, brief history and
description.

319. Mint Museum of Art.   Charlotte, N.C.   "Amish Quilts".   An-
      tiques Show Bulletin, 10th Anniv. Ed. , 1976, 31-35.
            Color cover: Sunshine and Shadow (c. 1930).   Five black-
and-white photos.   E. g. , Fans (1899), Sawtooth Diamond (1925), Star
(1850) and Diamond (1885).   Quilts are from the collection of Phyllis
Haders and date from 1850 to 1935.   Brief history of the Amish,
the rules of their faith and their quilts.   Also contains a short biographical sketch of Phyllis Haders.

320. Moore College of Art.   Pennsylvania Quilts: One Hundred
      Years 1830-1930.   Philadelphia: The College, 1978, unpged.
            Contains color and black-and-white photos of thirty-five
quilts, mostly Amish and Mennonite, pieced and appliquéd.   Examples: Amish Philadelphia Pavement, Star of Bethlehem, Log Cabin
Furrows, Drunkard's Path and crazy quilt.   Does not show all thirty-
five quilts.   Contains a bibliography.

321. Museum of North Orange County.   Orange County Quilts: A
      Decade of Transition 1972-1982.   Fullerton, Calif.:   The Mu-
      seum, 1982, brochure.
            Documents the exhibition of fifty-one quilts held from
October 5 through November 28, 1983.   Includes statements by Michael Mudd, museum director, and Hazel Hynds, curator.   Checklist
of quilts notes the artist, pattern name, provenance and size.

322. The New American Quilt.   Asheville, N. C.:   Lark Books,
      1981, 95pp.
            Compiled in conjunction with Quilt National.   Contains
over fifty color photos of original quilts that were winners of the
1979 and 1981 Quilt National at Athens, Ohio.   Gives quotes from
the artist about her quilt.   Shows both traditional quilts, and new
designs done with nonfabric materials.   Over 100 photos in all.   No
patterns.

323. Newman, Joyce.   North Carolina Country Quilts: Regional
      Variations.   Chapel Hill, N. C.:   The Ackland Art Museum,
      1978, 52pp.
            Documents show of sixteen quilts held from December
17, 1978 through January 21, 1979 at the William Hayes Ackland
Memorial Art Center.   Black-and-white photos of each quilt; color
cover.   Introduction by Evan H. Turner, director.   Essay on the

exhibit by the author.   The quilts are from three areas of North
Carolina illustrating certain regional quilting styles: 1.   Rowan-
Cabarrus Area; 2.   Perquimans-Chowan Area; 3.   Sampson-Duplin
Area.   Brief bibliography.   Each photo accompanied by pertinent
information and description.   Examples: Prairie Star (c. 1830),
Tulip Appliqué (c. 1845), Carpenter's Wheel (1858), Diamond Star
(nineteenth century), Sunburst (nineteenth century), and Checkerboard
(nineteenth century).   Also lists lenders to the show.

324.   North Carolina Museum of History.   Artistry in Quilts.   Ra-
        leigh, N. C.:   The Museum, 1975, 69pp.
               Exhibition catalog for show held from November 10, 1974
through January 19, 1975.   Covers three centuries of quilts emphasizing those made and used in North Carolina.   One hundred twenty
black-and-white photos.   Categories: 1.   Quilting (#1-13) whole-
cloth quilts; 2.   Piecework (#14-79); 3.   Appliqué (#80-110) and
Miscellaneous (#111-120).

325.   Oklahoma Historical Society.   A Century of Quilts from the
        Collection of the Oklahoma Historical Society.   Oklahoma City:
        The Society, 1981, 56pp.
               Catalog of twenty-seven color photos of quilts dating from
the nineteenth century to the 1930's and illustrating three techniques:
pieced, appliqué or combination--some with embroidery.   Includes
statement by Ronald Reeves, the former curator of collections at the
society.   The introduction by Margot L. Nesbitt, member of the
Board of Directors of the Museum and Historical Sites Commission
of the society discusses the Colonial period when quilts were linked
to the artists' homelands; Revolutionary period, where they display
French accents; Pioneer period; the Civil War (1850's-1860's) and
the centennial (1870's).   The annotations give pertinent information
on the quilts.   Examples: Rose of Sharon (early nineteenth century),
Flower Garden (early nineteenth century), North Carolina Lily
(c. 1860), Pine Burr (late nineteenth century) and Monkey Wrench
(early twentieth century).   Bibliography.

326.   Plews, Edith Rice.   Hawaiian Quilting on Kauai: An Address
        given to the Mokihana Club at Lihue, Kauai, March 1, 1933.
        Kauai, Hawaii: The Kauai Museum, 1976, 31pp.
               Catalog contains twenty-three black-and-white photos from
the 1933 show of 109 quilts exhibited at this club meeting.   Some of
these are now part of the Kauai Museum collection, some are privately owned.   Eight-page statement by Edith Plews reviews the
history of the art, technique and quilt names.   Examples of quilts:
Hawaiian Flag, Ka Pika Ohale Alii, Lily pattern, Breadfruit Leaf,
Pineapple, Helene's Lei and Grape Vine.

327.   Pottinger, David.   Quilts from the Indiana Amish.   New York:
        E. P. Dutton, 1983, 88pp.
               Documents the exhibition at the New York City Gallery
of the Department of Cultural Affairs held from June 28 through August 21, 1983, curated by David Pottinger and drawn from his gift
to the Museum of American Folk Art.   The Pottinger quilts are

from the Elkhart and LaGrange counties in Indiana, and date from
1870 through 1940. There are design examples of Fans, Bow Ties,
Lone Stars, Hole in the Barn Door, Log Cabins, Baskets and One-
Patch. Color photos of 138 quilts. Author notes that the use of
synthetic batt, larger scale and printed fabric around 1940 changed
the appearance of Amish quilts.

328. Pullman, Christopher and Pullman, Esther. American Quilts:
     The GE Gallery's Bicentennial Show. Fairfield, Conn.: Gen-
     eral Electric Co., 1976, 3pp.
         Catalog of twenty-three quilts shown at the General Elec-
tric Gallery in 1976. Small photos of each of the quilts accompanied
by quilt name, date and description. E. g., Sixteen-patch variation
(c. 1875), Four-Patch (c. 1925), Doll quilt (1860-70), LeMoyne Star
(1875), Lotus Flower (1865) and Lady of the Lake (1801). Quilts
are from the Pullman collection.

329. QSA Quilts 1981: Expressions in Blue and White. Greenburg,
     Pa.: The Westmoreland County Museum of Art, 1981, 5pp.
         Checklist of a show sponsored by the Quilting Society of
America. Category I: Blue and White (#1-88); II: Ecclesiastical
(#89-108). Checklist gives artist's name, city of residence, quilt
title, date, size and price, if it was for sale. Cover has blue-
and-white illustration of Birds in Flight pattern.

330. The Quilt Question: An Exhibition of Selected Traditional and
     Contemporary Quilts. Plymouth, Mass.: Ocean Spray Cran-
     berries, Inc., 1979, 14pp.
         Documents the show held at the Cranberry World Visitors'
Center from June 1 through June 2, 1979, curated by Anita Franks.
Twelve color photos of six traditional quilts from the Plymouth area
and six modern quilts by area textile artists. Examples: 1979
prizewinner in the National Cranberry Contest, Baby Sampler (c. 1870),
The Bear Necessities (1978) and Nancy and David (1977). Photos
accompanied by descriptive paragraph or two, size and owner's name.

331. Quilts: A Tradition in Southern Illinois. Chicago: Chicago
     Public Library, 1979, poster.
         Exhibition poster with reverse-side documentation of the
forty-three quilts in the show, dating from 1834 to 1979.
         Checklist notes name of quilt, date, artist and locale,
accompanied by a background paragraph. E. g., Granny's Dresses
(1979), Two Red Peacocks (1920), Feathered Star (1950), Postage
Stamp (1900), Walnut Blossom (1834) and Cluster of Stars (1870).
Fourteen black-and-white photos. Show ran from December 1, 1979
through February 3, 1980 at the Chicago Public Library Cultural
Center. The poster side shows a colored detail from Cherry Basket (1920). The exhibit was curated by Susan Kolojeski. Eight
slides (without sound) accompanied the exhibit.

332. Quilts: A Tradition of Variations. Albany, Calif.: The East
     Bay Heritage Quilters, 1982, 62pp.
         Catalog from an exhibit at Mills College Art Gallery,

Oakland, California, 1982. Forty-six black-and-white photos and twenty-eight color photos; color cover. Examples: Feathered Star, Bars, Irish Chain, Nine-Patch, Trees, Baskets, Log Cabin, School House, Diamonds and variations.

333. Quilts in the Garden Spot. Lancaster, Pa.: Privately printed, 1978, 6pp.
          This quilt show was held at the Old Courthouse in Lancaster, from July 16 through 29, 1978, in conjunction with the Lancaster Summer Arts Festival. No photos. Lists thirty-seven quilts (five Amish) with owner's name, brief description, history, size and date. E.g., Crib quilt, Variable Star pattern (c. 1850), Lancaster County Rose, Rose of Sharon and Orange Peel.

334. Rhode Island School of Design. Museum of Art. Mountain Artisans, an Exhibition of Patchwork and Quilting, Appalachia. Providence: RISD, 1970, 48pp.
          Documents the exhibit held at the museum from October 1 through 25, 1970. Black-and-white photos of eleven quilts from a show of twenty-one. Designs such as Granny's Flower Garden, Delectable Mountains, Drunkard's Path and Jacob's Ladder. Annotations to each quilt explain the Mountain Artisan's pattern and note color and derivation of the pattern name. Black-and-white photos of the Appalachian area and the local people; short history of the Mountain Artisans and of the art of quilting. Twenty-five-item bibliography. Essay "Waste Not Want Not," by Eleanor Fayerweather, curator of the Costume Center at the Rhode Island School of Design.

335. Robinson, Charlotte ed., The Artist and the Quilt. New York: Knopf, 1983, 144pp.
          This exhibition of twenty quilts ran from September 10 through October 22, 1983 at the McNay Art Institute in San Antonio. The quilts were shown in juxtaposition with the work of other artists. Essays on "American Quilts 1770-1880," by Jean Taylor Federico; "Geometry and Flowers," by Miriam Shapiro; "Up, Down, and Across," by Lucy Lippard; "Breaking Stars," by Eleanor Munro; "Design and Construction," by Bonnie Persinger and "The Quilt Project," by Charlotte Robinson. Quilts categorized as: 1. Overall pattern; 2. Figurative appliqué; 3. Feminist Collage; 4. Appliqué images repeated in photo transfer or painting and 5. miscellaneous abstract. Numerous black-and-white and color photos; black-and-white illustrations of design and construction. Biographical information on the artists and the quilters accompanied by their photos and a photo of the artwork. Includes index and note on the authors. Color cover. Some quilts pictured: Road to the Center of the World, by Alice Baber/Edith Mitchell; Patang, by Lynda Benglis/Amy Chamberlin; Sleep in the Arms of the Great Mother/Women Rising, by Marie Griffin Ingalls/Mary Beth Edelson; Fan Lady Meets Ruffled Waters, by Harmony Hammond/Bob Douglas; Starwort Phenomena, by Ellen Lanyon/Angela Jacobi and Variations of the Theme of Walking, by Isabel Bishop/Wenda Von Weise. The Artist and the Quilt collection is now owned by Phillip Morris Inc.

336. Santa Cruz County Art Museum. Amish Quilts. Santa Cruz,
      Calif.: The Museum, 1982, 3pp.
          Brochure/checklist of a show held from December 12,
1982 through January 30, 1983. Foreword by Robert McDonald.
Essay "Amish Quilts," by Edward Brown. Nine quilts from Lancaster County, Pennsylvania. Checklist notes quilt name, date,
fabric, size and owner's name. Two color photos: Bars (wool,
c. 1890) and Double Nine-Patch (wool, c. 1925).

337. Santa Rosa Quilt Guild. Festival of Quilts, 1978. Privately
      printed, 1978, 14pp.
          Checklist of 510 quilts in the first Festival of Quilts held
from April 21 through 23, 1978 at the Santa Rosa Fairgrounds. Information given includes quilt name, maker and size. Also notes
exhibitors' addresses.

338. _____. Festival of Quilts, 1983. Privately printed, 1983,
      27pp.
          Checklist of 451 quilts in the National Quilt Contest and
Exhibit held from May 20 through 22, 1983 at the Sonoma County
Fairgrounds, Santa Rosa, California. Information given: maker's
name, quilt name and size. Also includes names and addresses of
exhibitors.

339. Sears, Roebuck and Company. A Century of Progress in
      Quiltmaking. Chicago: Sears and Roebuck, 1934, 30pp.
          Published to celebrate the Chicago World's Fair in 1933
and the company's quilt contest.

340. Sheldon Memorial Art Gallery. University of Nebraska, Lin-
      coln. Quilts from Nebraska Collections. Lincoln: The Gallery,
      1974, 74pp.
          Catalog for an exhibition held from September 17 through
October 13, 1974 in collaboration with the Lincoln Quilters Guild.
Fifty-five photos in color, and black-and-white, of all the quilts in
the show. Some detail photos. The quilts date from the early 1800's
to 1974 and represent pieced and appliquéd work from Nebraska public
and private collections, many by natives of the state. Examples:
Star of Bethlehem, Rose Wreath, Log Cabin, Return of the Swallows,
Sunrise and Baby Blocks. Five quilts by Grace McCance Snyder.
The catalog lists the owner, maker and size and gives a description.
Color cover.

341. Shipley Art Gallery. Gateshead, England. Quilts from North-
      umberland and Durham. Gateshead, England: The Gallery,
      1980, 15pp.
          Twenty-six black-and-white photos of quilts from the show
held in 1980. Information: quilt style, date, size, maker's name,
lender's name, description and history. E.g., All-over quilt (c. 1820),
Basket quilt (early twentieth century) and True Lovers Knot (c. 1943).

342. Swan, Susan S. A Winterthur Guide to American Needlework.
      New York: Crown, for the Friends of the Henry du Pont Win-
      terthur Museum, 1976, 144pp.
            Guide to needlework examples at the museum, including
quilts and whitework. Arranged chronologically from 1650 to 1890.
Over 100 black-and-white photos. Sixteen color plates.

343. Textile Museum. Molas: Art of the Cuna Indians. Washing-
      ton, D. C.: The Museum, 1973, 27pp.
            Contains fifty-one black-and-white photos, and illustrations,
for a show held from April 3, 1973 through September 9, 1973 at
the Textile Museum, later circulated by the International Exhibitions
Foundation. Color cover. Lists the contributors to the show. Brief
discussion of the cultural background of the Cuna Indians. Examples:
Tropical Fish; Pelican; Coconut Palm; Palm Tree.

344. Thomas, Katheryn. "Quilts in the New York State Historical
      Association Collection." M. A. thesis. State University of
      New York College at Oneonta, 1977, 162pp.
            The purpose of the thesis was twofold: to learn more
about American quilts by looking at examples in the New York State
Historical Society collection, and to plan a book based on the research. Author surveyed the association's quilt collection and chose
thirty-nine quilts for their unique nature, their aesthetic value, the
quality of construction and the value of the quilt in the collection.
Pages xii-109 contain the layout of the proposed book. Introduction
discusses styles of quilts, construction, the quilt revival and the
evolution from whole-cloth to pieced tops. Includes glossary and a
thirty-six-item bibliography. Twenty-five black-and-white photos.
Annotations give pattern name, construction, date, size and descriptive paragraph. Most are thought to have originated in New York
State. E. g., Star of Bethlehem (nineteenth century), Whole-cloth
(1800), Windmill (nineteenth century), Lucy Day quilt, Tulip appliqué
(c. 1840), Grossman quilt (c. 1850) and Postage Stamp (nineteenth
century).

345. Victoria and Albert Museum. Department of Textiles. Notes
      on Applied Work and Patchwork. London: Her Majesty's Sta-
      tionery Office, 1938, 18pp. and plates.
            Shows the best examples in the museum. Discusses ap-
pliqué and its history. Examples: German wall hanging (fifteenth
century), French panel (1600), Persian prayer rug (nineteenth century), Hungarian woman's jacket (nineteenth century), English silk
patchwork coverlet, English coverlet with hexagons and applied border
(late eighteenth century) and Star of Bethlehem (U. S., late nineteenth century). Black-and-white photos of either the whole item or
a detail of it, with annotations.

346. _____. Notes on Quilting. London: Her Majesty's Station-
      ery Office, 1932, 14pp. with plates.
            Illustrates the best examples from the museum collection.
Black-and-white photos and a history of quilting. The examples are
annotated with pertinent information. Examples: Sicilian coverlet
(1400), Portuguese coverlet (seventeenth century), English white satin

jacket (late seventeenth century), English linen coverlet (1703), English silk pillow (early eighteenth century), English satin dress (early eighteenth century) and English linen chalice cover (about 1700).

347. Vlach, John Michael. The Afro-American Tradition in Decorative Arts. Cleveland: Cleveland Museum of Art, 1978, 175pp.
        This exhibition was held at the Cleveland Museum of Art from February 1 through April 2, 1978. Pages 43 to 75 are devoted to quilting. The catalog contains thirty black-and-white photos and five black-and-white illustrations. Discusses the quilts of Harriet Powers, with two photos of her quilts, and notes describing each block. Compares African appliquéd work to Afro-American quilts.

348. Weissman, Judith Reiter. "Anonymous Beauty: Quilts, Coverlets and Bedcovers--Textile Treasurers from Two Centuries." Clarion (Spring 1981), pp. 24-39.
        Exhibition catalog for the show held at the Museum of American Folk Art. Contains twenty-four black-and-white photos with descriptions. Also includes a checklist prepared by Penny M. Brickman of the quilts, coverlets, and bedcoverings in the museum's permanent collection. This inventory notes the quilt name, date, maker, style, fabric, description and history. Photo examples: Barn Raising (c. 1875); Double Wedding Ring (c. 1920); Bittersweet XII (1980), by Nancy Crow and Gingham Dog and Calico Cat crib quilt (c. 1910). The curator's statement reviews quilting in America, the social need for it, design, album quilts, appliqué and stenciling, and is accompanied by footnotes.

349. Wenham Museum. Contemporary Quilters. Wenham, Mass.: The Museum, 1980, 3pp.
        Mimeographed catalog of show held from May 18 through September 7, 1980 at the Wenham Museum. No photos. Lists twenty-six quilts with the artist's name, address, size of quilt and description (fabric, color and reverse of quilt). E. g., Barnboards, by Rhoda Cohen; Thy Kingdom Come, by Marie Kuperferman; Kaleidoscope, by Mary B. Golden; Broken Star, by Catherine Dwyer and Victorian Home, by Betty Hosford.

350. White, Margaret. Quilts and Counterpanes in the Newark Museum. Newark: The Museum, 1948, 90pp.
        First catalog of the museum's collection, now considered a reference work. Illustrations of items made between 1680 and 1900. Contains glossary and bibliography.

351. Winnipeg Art Gallery. Manitoba Quilts and Ceramics: A Survey of Contemporary Quilting and Pottery in Southern and Central Manitoba. Winnipeg: The Gallery, 1972, unpaged.
        Catalog for show held from October 7 through November 13, 1972. Black-and-white photos of some of the fifty pieced and appliquéd quilts, with artist and owner noted. Examples: Sunbonnet Sue, Butterflies, Grandmother's Flower Garden, Drunkard's Path and Variation of the Double Irish Chain.

352. Wolfe, Ruth. <u>Looking at American Quilts</u>. Wilton, Conn.:
      Wilton Historical Society, 1980, 10pp.
          Catalog of thirty-five quilts (one quilt frame) from an
exhibition held from June 2 through 15, 1980 to celebrate the seventy-
fifth anniversary of Richardson-Merrel Inc., a company in Wilton.
Seven-item glossary, brief bibliography and outline instructions with
illustrations for making a quilt. Essay on quilting by the curator,
Ruth Wolfe. Seven black-and-white photos of quilts, most loaned by
a private collector. Catalog lists quilts, and pertinent information.
E. g., Linsey-woolsey (eighteenth or early nineteenth century), Amish
Bars (early twentieth century), Orange Peel (nineteenth century),
Star of Bethlehem (second half nineteenth century) and Pinwheel Doll
quilt (late nineteenth century). Cover has six illustrations of patchwork block patterns. The show, entitled Great American Quilts at
the Museum, drew on examples from this show.

353. Woodard, Thomas K. and Greenstein, Blanche. "Hawaiian
      Quilts: Treasures of an Island Folk Art." <u>The Clarion</u> (Sum-
      mer 1979), pp. 16-27.
          Catalog of the show held at the Museum of American Folk
Art from July 3 to September 2, 1979. Lists the quilts with their
English and Hawaiian name, maker's name, fabric, place, date, size
and owner's name. Fifteen black-and-white photos. Examples: My
Beloved Flag (pre-1918), Grape Vine (pre-1918), Crowns (pre-1918)
and Bent Knee (early twentieth century). Essay by Woodard and
Greenstein relates the history of sewing and quilting on the Islands,
discusses color of the early quilts, distinguishing them from their
New England counterparts and notes their construction and design.
The twenty-four quilts in the show are from the Honolulu Academy
of Arts, the Bernice P. Bishop Museum and private collectors.

354. Worthing Museum and Art Gallery. <u>Sew to Bed</u>. Worthing,
      Sussex, England: The Museum, 1977, 11pp.
          Catalog of exhibit held from March 5 to April 23, 1977
at the Museum. Lists twenty quilts. No photos. Does not note
specific pattern name. Lists each quilt by style (patchwork, coverlet, etc.). Also includes a descriptive paragraph. Examples: patchwork quilt (1860; coverlet (late eighteenth century); patchwork bedspread
(late nineteenth century); printed bedcover (eighteenth century).

III. PERIODICAL ARTICLES

355.   Adams, Marie Jeanne. "Harriet Powers Pictorial Quilts."
       Black Art 3 (Summer 1978): 12-28.
              Photo of Mrs. Powers and black-and-white photos of her
first Bible quilt, now at the Smithsonian. Black-and-white photo of
her quilt at the Museum of Fine Arts, Boston, with a chart describing each block. Four color detail photos of various blocks. Color
photo of African appliquéd wall hanging. A show by the Cleveland
Museum of Art brought the two Powers' quilts together. Notes that
the quilts and the artist's descriptions are documents of black women
from those years. Gives the history of her Bible quilts and describes the blocks.

356.   "All-White Quilted Coverlet." Antiques 51 (Apr. 1947): 236-7.
              Frontispiece photo of a quilt dated 1841 from the collec-
tion of Neil C. Gest, with description. The quilt theme is the cam-
paign of Wm. Henry Harrison. A Log Cabin motif in the corners
dates the quilt to that era. Article notes that it is unusual to find
the Log Cabin and Cider Barrel motif together.

357.   Allen, Gwenfread E. "Quilts of Hawaii." Design 37 (Nov.
       1935): 16-18; 36.
              Compares the technique and design of Hawaiian and New
England quilts. Hawaiian quilt designs were influenced by the native
women's desire for dresses like the one worn by the missionary
women, and by the technique they had used in designing tapa cloth.
Their method of quilting was unique because it followed the pattern.
Historical events gave added inspiration to quiltmaking: the birth
of the Prince of Hawaii in 1858, the late-nineteenth-century overthrow
of the Hawaiian monarchy, giving rise to Royalist flag quilts and
the recent quilt revival. The author discusses the 1935 show at the
Honolulu Academy of Arts and popular designs.

358.   Alonso, Harriet. "Hawaiian Quilts: Treasures of an Island
       Folk Art." Fiberarts 6 (Nov. 1979): 77.
              Three black-and-white photos of Hawaiian quilts, one of
women quilting at the Mokihana Club in 1933. E. g., Crown and
Kahilis (1886), Beautiful Unequaled Gardens of Eden and Elenale
(n. d.) and My Beloved Flag (1918). Reviews the show at the Museum
of American Folk Art, New York City, held from July 3 to September 2, 1979. States that, in addition to a quilt show, the exhibit
was also a view of the history, culture and feelings of the quiltmakers. Gives a brief history of quiltmaking in the Islands. Discusses

some of the quilts in the show, their construction and the practice
of using other artists' patterns. The quilts illustrate the fusion of
of two cultures.

359. "American Patchwork Quilt."   American Fabrics 15 (1950):
      148-53.
            Nine black-and-white photos of quilts from the Brooklyn
Museum and from private collectors. Includes a reprint of an article from the December 2, 1877 issue of Harpers Weekly. Relates
the history of the United States to quilt designs. Includes a repro-
duction of the painting "The Quilting Party" (1840-50) at the Museum
of Modern Art.

360. "American Quilts on Exhibition." Antiques 53 (Apr. 1948):
      301.
            One black-and-white photo detail of a pictorial quilt dated
1847. Exhibition review of the show at the New York Historical
Society. Over fifty quilts dating from 1770-1944 from the society's
collection, the Hudson River Museum in Yonkers and from the Peto
collection.

361. "Appliquéd Bedcover c. 1800." Antiques 21 (Mar. 1932): 24.
            Black-and-white photo of a quilt constructed of appliquéd
chintz, flower cutouts and birds and trees on a white background,
size 10' 4" x 9' 4". From the collection of Katherine Hartshorne.
Diamond medallion center with a quilted vine.

362. Avery, Virginia. "Florence Peto--Renaissance Woman of Mid
      Century." Quilters Newsletter Magazine 11 (Jan. 1980): 16-
      18; 26.
            Photo of Mrs. Peto; six of her quilts pictured in color.
Relates how the author met Florence Peto and what she learned from
her. Description accompanies the photos. Biographical sketch.

363. _____. "A New Look at Trapunto." Quilter's Newsletter
      Magazine 10 (July 1979): 16-19.
            Color, and black-and-white photos. Description, history
and directions for trapunto.

364. "Baltimore Presentation Quilt 1847, From the Collection of
      Mrs. Florence Peto." Antiques 55 (June 1949): 424-5.
            Brief article describes the frontispiece: an autographed
Baltimore presentation quilt made in the 1840's and 1850's. Relates
the history of the quilt made for Rev. John G. Smart of the First
Presbyterian Church, Baltimore.

365. Bass, Ruth. "Exhibition Review: Edward Larson." Art News
      (Apr. 1981): 194.
            Edward Larson uses an "American" Theme for his quilts.
They are not intended to be utilitarian. Black-and-white photo of
the John Dillinger quilt (1979). The artist rides a line between art
and craft. From the show "Wood Toys, Woodcarvings & Picture
Quilts" at the Monique Knowlton Gallery, New York City.

366.   Bates, Kenneth.   "Connecticut River Quilt." House and Garden
        148 (Jan. 1976):   22.
                Black-and-white photo of the entire quilt.   Three black-
and-white photos of individual blocks.   Describes this bicentennial
quilt made by members of the Lyme Connecticut Craft Guild.   It is
comprised of twelve appliquéd and embroidered blocks: farms, a
local fair, Lyme Congregational Church, Essex boathouse, Baldwin
Bridge, Lyme Public Library, Saybrook Lighthouse, Gillette Castle and the opera house.

367.   Beam, Ethel.   "Streamlining the Art of Quilting." House
        Beautiful 98 (Aug. 1956):   74-77; 112.
                Includes ten photos.   Quiltmaking has become a lost art
because patterns became stereotyped.   Encourages the reader to be
creative.   Notes that hoops have replaced frames.   Four hints: use
original designs, work freehand and use dyes, make stitches larger
and use quilt to illustrate the present.   Photos of contemporary quilts.

368.   Beaudoin-Ross, Jacqueline.   "An Early Eighteenth-Century
        Pieced Quilt in Montreal." Canadian Art Review (RACAR)
        VI#2:   106-109.
                A scholarly article with four illustrations and footnotes.
The author, curator of costumes and textiles at the McCord Museum
in Montreal, analyszes an early silk pieced quilt in the collection
and determines it to be the "earliest known extant silk patchwork
quilt."   The author analyzes it on various levels--construction, design and fabric, the pattern of patchwork (Yankee Puzzle) of eighteenth century origin--and compares its method of construction to
three other quilts of an early date: 1785, late eighteenth century
and 1708.   She dates the fabric to the early eighteenth century by
comparing it to other quilts whose dates are known.   Sees it belong-
ing to the silk patchwork tradition.

369.   "Beautiful Christmas You Make Yourself--Gingham Patchwork."
        House and Garden   142 (Dec. 1972):   36-9.
                Color photos of a wreath, tablecloth, angels, stockings
and a patchwork tree.   Gives descriptions and brief directions.

370.   "Bed of Flowers." American Home   79 (March 1976):   48-9.
                Quilted comforter made from scarves.   Directions for
making the quilt by sewing scarves together, accompanied by photo
of the quilt.   Notes materials needed and procedure, including binding.   Black-and-white illustration of construction.   Product information p. 92.

371.   "Bedcover with Chintz Appliqué. Ohio Quilt; Quilt with Ap-
        pliqué and Embroidery." Antiques   17 (Jan. 1930):   26-8.
                Black-and-white photos of: 1.   chintz appliqué bedcover
(early eighteenth century) with a short description; 2.   an Ohio quilt
(c. 1835) and 3.   a quilt with appliqué and embroidery (c. 1835).

372.   Benberry, Cuesta.   "Afro-American Women and Quilts." Un-
        coverings   1 (1980):   64-67.

Essay on quilts made by black women and those made about Afro-Americans by white women.

373. _____. "The 20th Century's First Quilt Revival." Quilter's Newsletter Magazine 10 (July 1979): 20-22.
First in a three-part series on the quilt revival. Examines patterns and quilts created between 1890 and the 1930's. Illustrations of block patterns. Reviews publications devoted to quiltmaking.

374. _____. "The 20th Century's First Quilt Revival." Quilter's Newsletter Magazine 10 (Sept. 1979): 25-26; 29.
One color photo. Part Two of a three-part series. Discusses the first quilt revival of 1910 and events that preceded it.

375. _____. "The 20th Century's First Quilt Revival." Quilter's Newsletter Magazine 10 (Oct. 1979): 10-11; 37.
Three black-and-white photos. Part Three in a three-part series. Discusses the years surrounding World War I. Concludes with a bibliography of books, periodicals and catalogs from those years.

376. Berman, Linda and Berman, Irwin. "Collecting Children's Quilts: The Lure of the Chase." The Clarion (Summer 1979): 40-5.
Nine black-and-white photos. Photo annotations include quilt name, locale, date, size and brief description. E.g., Log Cabin (c. 1870), Lady in the Lake (c. 1915), Hat & Heart (c. 1850) and Rooster crazy quilt (c. 1880). Authors describe how they started their collection, the pitfalls they encountered and some of the examples shown in the article. They also discuss the process of going to shows and auctions, contacting dealers and how to care for quilts.

377. Block, Jean Libman. "A Quilt is Built: Exhibition at the Museum of Contemporary Crafts." Craft Horizons 36 (Apr. 1976): 30-5.
Review of the show The New American Quilt held from April 1 to June 13, 1976 at the Museum of Contemporary Crafts. Reviews the work of contemporary fabric artists exhibiting in this show. Color cover: Puzzle of the Floating World No. 3, by Katherine Westphal. Thirty-eight works exhibited. Seven black-and-white photos; three color photos. E.g., Dream Quilt: One Man's Nantucket, by Wenda von Weise; American Velvet Lady, by Nancy Helfant; Pine Winter, by Molly Upton; Hands & Feet, by Cynthia Panucci; Flying Carpet #2, by Anne Raymo and Mountain from My Window, by Helen Bitar.

378. Bonfield, Lynn A. "The Production of Cloth, Clothing, and Quilts in 19th-Century New England Homes." Uncoverings 2 (1981): 77-96.
Author relies on diaries from the nineteenth century to illustrate the way women spent their time, with an emphasis on needlework. Footnotes.

379.   Bordes, Marilynn. "Baltimore Album Quilts." Connoisseur
       207 (June 1981):   80.
              Exhibition Review: Metropolitan Museum of Art, June
30 to August 30, 1981.   Black-and-white photo of a friendship quilt
(c. 1850).   States that these quilts in their color, design, detail
and needlework represent the highpoint of the appliqué coverlet in
America.   The 1974 show at the Metropolitan, 12 Great Quilts from
the American Wing, raised questions about these quilts, artists,
fabric and sources of design.   States that through detailed research,
Dena Katzenberg and her staff have answered these questions.   This
show has twenty-four of the finest Baltimore album quilts known.
The curators have researched the quilts, quiltmakers, Baltimore
history and textile sources.

380.   Bowen, Helen. "The Ancient Art of Quilting." Antiques   3
       (Mar. 1923):   113-117.
              Contains five black-and-white photos.   E. g., candlewick
spread, Boulder, Colo.; whole-cloth quilt with feather, pineapple,
and ocean wave design, Nine-Patch (1870's); silk whole cloth with
feather pattern (eighteenth century); all-over quilt (1749) with an
Oriental pattern.   Refutes the idea that quilting had died out and that
it is purely an American craft.   Discusses categories of quilting
patterns.   E. g., straight line, curved line, shell and fan.   Describes
the items illustrated.

381.   _____.   "Corded and Padded Quilting." Antiques 6 (Nov.
       1924):   250-53.
              Laments that this technique has fallen from use.   De-
scribes the illustrations, the technique, owner and history.   Examples are from the Wadsworth Atheneum, the Essex Institute and private collectors.   One detail photo shows the stages of progress in
the unfinished piece.   Another photo shows an Oriental influence,
although the process is English.
              Figure 5 illustrates a Persian influence.   Five black-and-
white photos in all.

382.   Brackman, Barbara. "Charlotte Jane Whitehall--Appliqué Art-
       ist." Quilter's Newsletter Magazine 11 (Apr. 1980):   23-25;
       28, 31.
              Seven black-and-white photos of Mrs. Whitehall's quilts.
Biographical sketch of the artist.   Directions and patterns for Oriental Poppy Quilt made by her in 1937.

383.   _____.   "The Hall/Szabronski Collection at the University
       of Kansas." Uncoverings 3 (1982):   59-74.
              Contains two black-and-white photos.   Reviews these quilt
and book collections at the Helen F. Spencer Museum of Art.   Appendix notes the missing blocks from the Hall collection and where
a comparable photograph can be found in her book; Appendix II notes
the books, patterns and periodicals in the collection.   Text accompanied by footnotes.

384. _____. "Midwestern Pattern Sources." Uncoverings 1
(1980): 3-12.
      Reviews commercial pattern sources published during the
twentieth century, specifically Capper's Weekly and The Workbasket.
Bibliography of pamphlets and patterns from these two publications.

385. _____. "Quilts at the Chicago World's Fairs." Uncoverings
2 (1981): 63-75.
      Includes one black-and-white photo. Author contrasts the
Chicago World's Fair of 1893 and the 1933 Chicago World's Fair.
The article is the result of her search for the prizewinning quilts
from these fairs. Appendix lists the quilts she found that were en-
trants. Also lists the maker's name, quilt description and place of
origin. Accompanied by footnotes.

386. Bradley, Ann B. "Color Your World with Quilts." American
Home 77 (Sept. 1974): 66-9; 92-93.
      Color photos of a memory quilt, a sampler wall hanging
(where to order the kit) Courthouse Square and Baskets quilts (where
to send for instructions) and appliquéd ginghams with instructions (p. 92).
Gives materials needed and procedure involved.

387. _____. "Make Our Classic Square by Square Quilt." Ladies' Home Journal 9 (Aug. 1981): 88-9; 120.
      Two pages of color photos of the quilt on bed. Black-
and-white diagram of one quarter of the quilt. Gives fabric requirements, directions on cutting, assembling and finishing.

388. _____. "Quilt Craft: Quick, Easy, Fun." Ladies' Home
Journal 97 (May 1980): 108-9; 177.
      Two pages of color photos of finished projects involving
painting fabric and stitching around the design. Page 179 gives general directions, fabric requirements, how to enlarge the design shown,
transfer the design and paint it with acrylic or textile paint. Directions for a placemat, hot pad, pillows and wall hanging.

389. _____. "Stitch a Pillow Patchwork Quilt." American Homes
78 (Mar. 1975): 50-1.
      Color photo of a quilt with large squares stuffed and
stitched together. Directions on p. 76 give the finished size, fabric
needed and procedure involved.

390. Brightbill, Dorothy L. "Friendship Quilt You Can Make."
American Home 64 (Feb. 1961): 19-20.
      Photo of a friendship quilt based on one in the Shelburne
Museum collection. The one pictured is cross-stitched. Author
mentions the kit available from the magazine.

391. _____. "Make an Heirloom LeMoyne Star Quilt." American Home 75 (Oct. 1972): 148.

Full-size patterns for making a LeMoyne Star quilt.
Notes materials needed, procedure and finishing technique.

392.   Brown, Bertha. "Molas: The Geometry of Background Fill."
       Uncoverings 3 (1982): 13-23.
              Written by an anthropologist.   Includes six black-and-
white illustrations of molas.   In-depth discussion on the construction
of molas.   Bibliography and footnotes.

393.   Brown, Jo Geise.   "Notes on Fashion Institute of Technology's
       Presentation of Anonymous Beauty: Quilts, Coverlets and Bed
       Covers--Textile Treasures from Two Centuries, in Conjunction
       with the Museum of American Folk Art."   The Clarion (Spring/
       Summer 1981):   40-43.
              The author was the curator for the Fashion Institute of
Technology portion of the exhibit.   Four black-and-white photos:
Trapunto crib quilt (c. 1820); Grandmothers Flower Garden (c. 1840),
detail; Star variation (1870) and Amish Floating Bars (1920).   The
show was jointly presented by the Museum of American Folk Art
and the Fashion Institute of Technology.   The institute's exhibit of
about sixty quilts emphasized the "texture in design" of nineteenth-
and twentieth-century quilts.   Notes the effect created by stuffed work,
background quilting and the use of different fabric in the same quilt.

394.   Burrows, Fredrika Alexander.   "Old Fashioned Quilts."
       Hobbies 85 (May 1980): 60-1.
              Includes black-and-white photos of Wagon Wheel, detail of
mosaic, Double Star, Log Cabin; crazy and Barn Raising patterns.
Cover photo of Virginia Windflower.   Author discusses the social
function of the quilting bee, describing when and how it took place.
Discusses how a quilt is made along with quilt names relating to
religion, occupations, politics, the sun, stars and album quilts.
Describes a historical quilt in the Ford Museum which recounts the
history of the state of Oklahoma on the quilt top.   Talks about the
functional and aesthetic aspects of quilts.

395.   Butler, Joseph J.   "Great American Cover-Up: Counterpanes
       of the 18th and 19th Centuries."   Connoisseur 179 (Feb. 1972):
       135-6.
              Exhibition review.   Three black-and-white photos: album
quilt (1852), Pinwheel quilt (1840) and Jacquard coverlet (1850).   The
show had approximately 100 examples of needlework and weaving,
including a Calimanco quilt dated 1750 and several album quilts.
Mrs. Dena S. Katzenberg organized the exhibition which served as
an introduction to the Baltimore Museum of Art's collection.

396.   "Buying Quilt Fabrics by Mail."   Better Homes & Gardens
       55 (Apr. 1977): 79; 81.
              Mail-order houses fall into two categories: those with
samples available and those without.   The latter are known as grab-
bag orders.   Mail-order samples are similar to a fabric club: members receive swatches.   All the member pays is an enrollment fee.
Discusses ordering from fabric stores, noting that some have

authentic reproductions of old prints. Advises ordering fabric from
the samples in hand because of the difficulty in making accurate
judgments based on a photo. Advises testing fabric samples for
washability, shrinkage, color fastness (tells how to check for), fad-
ing, loose weave and wrinkle resistance. Grab-bag orders are sold
by the pound. The customer does not always know what he/she is
getting. These fabrics may be good for appliqués. The buyer may
expect three to four yards of cotton per pound, two yards of heavy
fabric per pound. Article lists nine mail-order suppliers.

397. Callum, Myles. "Southwest Quilters." Better Homes & Gar-
      dens 54 (Feb. 1976): 68-75.
           Written in cooperation with Patricia Cooper and Norma
Buferd, authors of The Quilters. Eight pages of color photos of
quilts made by quilters from the southwest: Pinwheel, Star of Bethlehem, Log Cabin, Little Baskets, Nine-Patch, simple block quilt,
Butterflies and Dresden Plate, with quotes by some of the quilters.
Bicentennial quilt pictured on the cover. Where to order material
noted on p. 117.

398. Chamberlain, Georgia. "Collect Sunbonnet Babies." Hobbies
      58 (Jan. 1954): 80-81.
           Historical discussion of the Sunbonnet Babies motif, dec-
orating items such as china, candlesticks, etc. Discusses Sunbonnet
Babies Primer by Eulalie Osgood and the Overall Boys.

399. "Chintz Patchwork and Appliqué Bedcover." Antiques 32
      (Oct. 1937): 174.
           Contains a black-and-white photo of an early-nineteenth-
century quilt made in South Carolina. It was one of six listed in
the inventory, dated 1846, of John White. From the collection of
J. Hamlin White.

400. "Christmas with Quilts in an Antique House." House and Gar-
      den 148 (Dec. 1976): 108-11.
           Four pages of color photos of quilts in the vacation house
of Richard and Phyllis Haders. E. g., Feathered Star, Rose of
Sharon, Streak of Lightning and Diamonds in a Square.

401. Cooper, Clare. "Collecting Quilts." Connoisseur 207 (June
      1981): 140-1.
           Article on the Jane Kasmin collection of English quilts
with some American, Canadian and Welsh examples. Color photos
of: 1. English Log Cabin (20th century); 2. 1930's English Fan
quilt; 3. nineteenth-century English military quilt made from old
uniforms and a blanket and 4. nineteenth-century American Pinwheel,
early nineteenth century English Tumbling Blocks; nineteenth-century
Square in the Middle quilt. The exhibition was held at Co-Existence,
2 Conduit Bldgs., Floral Street, Covent Garden, London.

402. Cooper, Emmanuel. "Irish Patchwork Exhibit 1800-1900."
      Art and Artist 14 (April 1980): 50.
           Exhibition review of a show at Somerset House, London,

in February 1980. Reviews the history of quiltmaking in Ireland
and distinguishes between the quilts made by the landlords and those
made by the tenants. Mentions notable pieces in the show.

403.   Cooper, Patricia. "Patchwork of the Pioneer West." Historic
        Preservation 31 (Mar. 1979): 12-17.
            Includes seven color photos of quilts. E.g., Windmill
Blades (1875), Prosperity is Just Around the Corner and Sunflower
(1940). Quilt designs were inspired by the quilter's environment.
The author uses experiences gained from writing The Quilters. Her
conversations with women in the southwestern United States told the
story of how they conquered their environment. The evolution of the
quilt reflects this progress: Windmills, Log Cabins, Furrows, Roads,
Houses and Flower Gardens, Town and Community.

404.   Corbin, Patricia. "Notes to Help You Decorate it Yourself."
        House and Garden 142 (Oct. 1972): 12, 16, 20.
            A directory of where to have items machine quilted, where
to buy quilt patterns, quilting thread, frames, how to care for quilts
and where to buy quilts. Notes the fairs, craft groups, antique dealers, books and magazines on quilting and where to enroll in classes.

405.   "Country Christmas Quilt Patterned Packages & Fanciful Dec-
        orations From Gingham and Calico." Better Homes & Gardens
        53 (Dec. 1975): 60-1; 19.
            Color photos and directions for Christmas Package Ban-
ner, Stuffed Angels, Patchwork-Pattern Gift Wrap, Soft Sculpture and
Tree. Gives fabric requirements and step-by-step instructions.
Black-and-white diagrams of reduced-size cutouts.

406.   "Country Stars." Good Housekeeping 187 (Aug. 1978): 118-
        21; 204.
            Four color photos of four prizewinners from Good House-
keeping's Great Quilt Contest: 1. Five-Star quilt by Vickie Milton
(Texas State winner); 2. Flower Basket by Wanda Dawson (Nebraska);
3. Sun Set Sea by Margaret Boesch (Rhode Island) and 4. Kentucky
Lily by Lucille Cox.

407.   "Cover: Quilt from Hawaiian Island with Breadfruit Design."
        Antiques 35 (May 1939): 223.
            Color cover of the quilt (c. 1830). Description on p. 223.
The author compares it to an illustration of the breadfruit plant.
Owner noted.

408.   "Coverlets & Quilts from Newark Museum Collections." An-
        tiques 51 (May 1947): 332.
            One black-and-white photo--center detail of a quilt (late
eighteenth century). Exhibition review of a show at the Newark Museum, with a brief history and description of the quilts shown.

409.   Cozart, Dorothy. "Women and Their Quilts as Portrayed by
        Some American Authors." Uncoverings 2 (1981): 19-33.
            Bibliographic essay on quilters as portrayed in American

fiction, from a story in Godey's Lady's Book in 1849, to a story in
Redbook in 1974. Accompanied by footnotes and a selected bibliography.

410. "Craft Comeback, Folk Art, Decorative Inspiration: The All-
      American Patchwork Quilt." House and Garden 142 (Oct.
      1972): 114-17.
            Four pages of color photos of Holstein/van der Hoof
quilts, Straight Furrows, Nine-Patch, New Jersey quilt (1880), Star
of Bethlehem and friendship quilt. Their collection has been exhibited at The Whitney, The Louvre during the summer of 1971 and at
the Renwick Gallery of the Smithsonian. Also includes; Sawtooth
(Pa. 1860-70), Flower Basket, Barn Raising, Baby's Blocks (N. J.
1930) and Garden of Eden (Pa. 1880).

411. "Craze for Quilts." Life 72 (May 1972): 74-80.
            News article on the quilt craze sparked by the 1971 show
at the Whitney. Eight pages of color photos of crazy quilt (Pa. 1850),
Double Wedding Ring (1870), Log Cabin (1850), Square Patch (1875),
crazy quilt (1875), Rainbow Stripes (1860) and photos of contemporary
quilts such as 109 Views, by Joyce Wieland. Baby Blocks quilt,
over 100 years old has 359 autographs of statesmen, authors, gen-
erals, scientists, churchmen and Abraham Lincoln. Quilts are from
the Holstein Collection and the Baltimore Museum of Art.

412. "Create a Quilt Big or Little." Good Housekeeping 170 (Feb.
      1970): 110-11.
            Color photo of an Eight-Point Star crib quilt and an Or-
ange Peel design. Patterns and directions are in a booklet available from the magazine. Ordering information on p. 146.

413. Cross, Mary. "The Quilts of Grant Wood's Family and Paint-
      ings." Uncoverings 3 (1982): 101-113.
            Includes five black-and-white photos and an illustration of
the Wood family tree. Describes six Wood family quilts. Also examines quilts in the paintings of Grant Wood. The article is foot-
noted with a bibliography, a list of museum collections and a list of
persons interviewed.

414. _____. "Researching Quilts in the Life of Grant Wood."
      Quilter's Newsletter Magazine 14 (Nov./Dec. 1983): 38-40.
            Six color and one black-and-white photo. Relates the
author's search for Grant Wood's family quilts and his paintings depicting quilts.

415. Davidson, Ruth Bradbury. "American Quilts." Antiques 55
      (Feb. 1949): 142.
            Book review of American Quilts by E. W. Robertson,
1948. The book draws conclusions about early American life by
studying old quilts. Includes short account of the textile industry.
Notes the factors that influenced quilt design.

416. Davis, Marilyn P. "The Contemporary American Quilter: A
      Portrait." Uncoverings 2 (1981): 45-51.

An anthropologist discusses the results of her survey of who quilts and why.

417.   Davis, Mildred J.   "Textiles in the Valentine Museum."
        Antiques 103 (Jan. 1973): 175-83.
              States that the Textile Resources and Research Center
"... has one of the largest collections of bed coverings in America.
Examples of appliqué, quilt, patchwork ... and embroidery." Good
examples from the South.   Generally reviews the collection of the
Textile Museum including lace, costume and sewing tools.   Photos:
an embroidered coverlet (c. 1775), a quilted bed cover from Virginia (mid-nineteenth century) and a coverlet with appliqué, embroidery and patchwork (late eighteenth century).

418.   DeGraw, Imelda G.   "Museum Quilt Collecting." Uncoverings
        2 (1981): 105-110.
              Describes the quilt collection of the Denver Art Museum,
especially the Charlotte Jane Whitehall quilts. Notes the importance
of artifact donations, loans and documentation to a museum.   Includes
two black-and-white photos: Single Tulip (c. 1825) and Flowers.

419.   deJulio, Mary. "A Record of a Woman's Work--The Betsey
        Reynolds Voorhees Collection." Uncoverings 3 (1982): 75-85.
              Three black-and-white photos.   The article states that
women needleworkers sewed various types of objects.   The author
has examined the Voorhees collection and finds a common style to
it, one that reflects its time and place.   Three black-and-white
photos.

420.   "Decorating the County Way with Fabulous Quilts."   Good
        Housekeeping 189 (Sept. 1979): 114-19.
              Color photos of quilts in the home of Phyllis Haders.
E. g., Mariner's Compass, Variable Star, Lone Star, Sunshine and
Shadow, Baby Blocks, Log Cabin, Ocean Wave cradle quilt, Triple
Irish Chain, Streak o'Lightning and a baby quilt in the Basket pattern.

421.   "Decorating with Quilts: Three All-American Ways in Red,
        White, and Blue Patchwork." Good Housekeeping 143 (Feb.
        1973): 58-9.
              Three color photos of quilts from the collection of Rhea
Goodman at the Quilt Gallery, 55 E. 86th St., N. Y.   Some of these
are also pictured in America's Quilts and Coverlets, by Safford and
Bishop.   E. g., Feathered Star with Flying Geese, Variable Star,
Double Irish Chain, Triple Irish Chain, Mariner's Compass, Pinwheel of Stars, Ocean Waves, Star of Bethlehem, Delectable Mountain and Streak of Lightning.   Gives address of Stearns & Foster
for ordering a pattern catalog.   The Goodman collection may be seen
by appointment.

422.   Dennis, Landt. "Comeback of the Quilt." Reader's Digest
        102 (Mar. 1973): 35-6.
              Five color photos from the Holstein collection: Square
Patch (N. J. 1875), Rainbow (Pa. 1860), crazy (Pa. 1850), album

and detail (Md. 1852). News item on the quilt revival with quotes from an executive at Stearns & Foster and the editor of Quilter's Newsletter Magazine. Gives examples of people starting classes and various cooperatives that have sprung up e. g. , Mountain Artisans (W. Va.) and Cabin Creek Quilts (W. Va.). Quotes Rhea Goodman and notes the Whitney show in 1971. Sketches quiltmaking history from its beginnings in the Orient to the present.

423. Dubois, Jean. "Crazy Quilt: A Collage in Color." Design
      77 (Fall 1975): 6-8.
          Includes five black-and-white photos of embroidery on a nineteenth-century quilt from Nevada. E. g. , frog, urn, man, flowers and a girl. States that the crazy quilt is enjoying new popularity because of a variety of design techniques and ease of assembly. Discusses fabrics used by the Victorians. Embroidery was used to delineate structure and emboss pictures. The author believes some of the designs found in old crazies were iron-on transfers. Gives her ideas on how the older techniques can be updated in modern work. Tells how to make a crazy quilt. Tells how various fabrics will adapt to his technique. In earlier times they were vehicles to display the artist's embroidery skills and were used as bed coverings or lap robes. Now they are hung as artwork.

424. Duprey, Martha. "Quilt Exhibition." Harriton Association
      Bulletin. Curator's Quarterly Report. 3 no. 1 (Spring 1979):
      3.
          Exhibition review of a show held April 21, 22, 1979. Fifty contemporary and antique quilts. Discusses four of the quilts in the show that were from the collection of the Harriton Association: a printed pattern on linen, a Variable Star baby quilt; a Nine-Patch and Flying Geese, from the last quarter of the nineteenth century. Includes two black-and-white photos: a contemporary quilted jacket and a printed linen quilt, dated 1781.

425. Dyer, Carolyn. "Small Endearments: 19th-Century Quilts
      for Children & Dolls." Fiberarts 8 (May/June 1981): 18-19.
          The show Small Endearments took three years to produce. A symposium was held in October 1979 for collectors and scholars that helped to create a network for this show. One hundred ninety-three quilts were exhibited at the Los Angeles Municipal Art Gallery. Includes a color photo of Basket and Flowers (c. 1850) and a black-and-white photo of the curator, Sandi Fox, with a crib quilt of her own design.

426. Eanes, Ellen F. "Nine Related Quilts of Mecklenburg County,
      North Carolina, 1800-1810." Uncoverings 3 (1982): 25-42.
          Three black-and-white quilt photos. One illustration of a map of Mecklenburg County 1789. Analysis and description of these quilts and a discussion of the family background of their makers. Many are now privately owned. Some are in the Mint Museum of History in Charlotte. Includes footnotes.

427. Einstein, Susan, photographer, and Pottinger, David, (Foreword). "Amish Interiors." The Quilt Digest (1983): 14-23.

Nine black-and-white photos of the interiors of Amish homes. E.g., a sewing corner, an enclosed porch, a dining room, bedroom, washroom, a placesetting for a wedding table with church benches set up, a boys room and a livingroom.

428.   "Feathered Star Quilt." Antiques 60 (Oct. 1951): 333.
        Picture and news item on a red-and-white patchwork quilt (c. 1840), recently given to the Wadsworth Atheneum by Ann Jennet Mitchell of Connecticut.

429.   Federico, Jean T. "White Work Classification System."
        Uncoverings 1 (1980): 68-71.
        Describes various types of white work using examples from the D. A. R. collection. Seeks to define candlewick, embroidery and stuffed work.

430.   Ferry, Christine. "To Quilt is Smartly Modern." Better
        Homes & Gardens 18 (Apr. 1940): 82-4.
        One black-and-white photo and one black-and-white illustration. General instructions for using the sewing machine to quilt. How to make templates, how to cut fabric and appliqué. General instructions for diamonds, rectangles and clamshells.

431.   Finch, Joyce H. "Design your own Historical Quilt." De-
        sign 78 (Midwinter 1977): 2-6.
        Discusses a group project for a historical quilt. Being part of a group endeavor can be as satisfying as the old-time barn raising or quilting parties. Gives ideas on how to initiate a community quilt. It can tell a story or show local landmarks. Notes the need for subgroups to design the quilt, while keeping in mind the entire project. Relates how a star quilt was made. Kits were made for the individual craftswomen, giving them background fabric, embroidery thread and material for appliqué. One person should sew all the blocks together. Another group does the quilting. Contains three black-and-white photos.

432.   Flynn, Mary. "Quilts from Kansas." Connoisseur 207 (July
        1981): 158.
        Reviews a show of twenty-five nineteenth-century quilts on loan from the Helen Foresman Spencer Museum of Art. Exhibition was held at the Neuberger Museum, New York City, from April to August 1981. Good examples of the design and technique developed by pioneer women.

433.   Fox, Sandi. "The Log Cabin: An American Quilt of the West-
        ern Frontier." The Quilt Digest (1983): 6-13.
        Five color photos, one in black and white; footnotes. Compares the development of the Log Cabin quilt design to the social evolution of families on the American frontier. Draws a line of pattern development from the basic Log Cabin, Barn Raising, Straight Furrow, Rail Fence, Zigzag, Courthouse Steps and the symbol of Hospitality: the Pineapple. Sees this trend running parallel to westward migration and the mythic beliefs of the American frontier in the nineteenth century.

434. "From All Across the Land: 51 Prize-Winning Quilts." Good
Housekeeping 186 (Mar. 1978): 124-135.
Each page full of color photos of winners from Good
Housekeeping's Great Quilt Contest. Directions for the first prize-
winner and four others on p. 218. Gives general directions and
specific directions for: Quilted Montage, Confetti, Sunburst, Ray
of Light, Engagement Ring and Hats & Patches. Some have reduced
diagrams. The quilts are categorized by locale: Midwest, Far
West and East. Where to order patchwork primer kit and Good
Housekeeping needlework kits, p. 210.

435. Galbraith, Etelka C. "Quilts: An American Craft." Design
37 (Dec. 1935): 25-8.
Discusses the importance of the stars, the sun and other
celestial bodies in quilt pattern names. E. g., Rainbow and Streak
O'Lightning. Illustrations of Feathered Star and Blazing Star. Discusses various patterns using examples. General discussion of the
need for harmony in the entire quilt when piecing and quilting.

436. Garoutte, Sally. "California's First Quilting Party." Uncoverings 2 (1981): 53-62.
Relying on diaries and histories of the times, the author
reconstructs the scenes surrounding a quilting party known to have
taken place in 1846 in California. Includes footnotes.

437. _____. "Early Colonial Quilts in a Bedding Context." Uncoverings 1 (1980): 18-27.
Examines inventories of homes in Colonial times to refute
the theory that quilts were readily found in early households and that
they were practical items only. Contains a bibliography and a graph
illustration.

438. _____. "Marseilles Quilts and Their Offspring." Uncoverings 3 (1982): 115-134.
Examines the origin of these whole cloth, stuffed or
corded quilts. Traces their route to America, the use of the loom
and their evolution in design. Footnotes. Fourteen black-and-white
photos.

439. Glover, Flavin. "Regarding the Discovery of the Cedar
Heights Quilt Collection in Lower Chattahoochee Valley, Ala-
bama." Uncoverings 2 (1981): 35-43.
Description of eighteen quilts found at the Cedar Heights
Plantation. Brief family history of the quilters who have lived in
the house. Footnotes. One black-and-white illustration.

440. Gough, Marion. "Quilts as Bedspreads." House Beautiful
89 (Feb. 1947): 78-81.
Color, and black-and-white photos of a large quilt cut
in two and put on twin beds, an appliquéd Oak Leaf, Flower Basket
and Eight-Point Star quilts. Decorating ideas given for the quilts
photographed.

441. "Grand Old Art of Quilting with a Young Look." Redbook
      140 (Mar. 1973): 104-11.
            Five photos: Log Cabin (McCall's Pattern), an All-Hex
quilt (Pa. Dutch), Virginia Reel, Dahlia and motif from Stars of
Alabama (Directions p. 155). Where to order Pennsylvania Dutch
pillow kits from Stearns & Foster, p. 144.

442. "Graphic Color of Quilts in an All White Room." House and
      Garden 150 (Oct. 1978): 142-3.
            Two pages of color photos of quilts on the walls of Mr.
and Mrs. Richard Haders' city apartment. Examples of Sunshine &
Shadow, The Diamond, Nine-Patch and others.

443. Gross, Joyce R. "Four Twentieth Century Quiltmakers."
      Uncoverings 1 (1980): 28-40.
            Biographical sketches of quiltmakers using original sources:
Myrtle M. Fortner, Jeannette D. Throckmorton, Bertha Stenge
and Florence Peto.

444. Gutcheon, Beth. "Quick Stitch Quilt." House and Garden 151
      (Jan. 1977): 106-7; 138.
            Color photos of quilts used as a tablecloth, wall banner
and bedcover. How to create a quilt using a kit from Gutcheon
Patchworks in the Lightning pattern. Tips on how to sew and piece
a quilt quickly. Photos of sewing, pressing, finishing and quilting.
Shopping information on p. 138.

445. _____. "Quilt National '79." Fiberarts 6 (Sept. 1979):
      80-2.
            Four color photos; five black-and-white photos including
Log Cabin variation, by Maria McCormick Snyder; Maine Quilt, by
Rhoda Cohen and Fences, by Virginia Randles. Color photos of
Earth Water Air & Fire, by Radka Donnell; Straight Furrows in
Geological Time, by Wenda F. von Weise; January, by Nancy Crow
and Flying Carpet, by Nancy Halpern. Quilt National '79 exhibited
fifty-six traditional designs by forty-four artists. Compares some
of the quilts to a style such as Art Deco and the paintings of Paul
Klee and Franz Kupka. Questions whether initial slide viewing by
judges accurately represents the finished quilt.

446. Hagood, Carol Cook. "Thimble by Thimble: A Collector's
      Quilt." Decorating & Craft Ideas 14 (July 1983): 64-65.
            Color photo of a white-worked quilt illustrating the use
of thimble designs in quilting. Photos of the thimble collection of
Lois Ide, a needlewoman who used eighteen of these designs to
create a quilt using dimensional appliqué, trapunto and embroidery.
Won "best of show" at Stanley Hywet Stitchery Showcase in Akron,
Ohio 1982.
            The quilt was shown in September 1983 in A World of Quilts
at Meadowbrook Hall, Rochester, Mich., a display of over 100 quilts.
The magazine has derived a Cupid & Garlands Thimble pillow and
includes directions. Gives cutting guides and shopping information.

447. Hall, Sally. "Quilt Resource Sampler." Fiberarts 8: 10-12.
        News items on such things as PBS-TV quiltmaking show,
a short synopsis of quilting books, a list of twenty-four periodicals,
conferences, guilds and brief paragraph on miscellany related to
quilts.

448. "Handquilting, a Craft Deluxe in the Hands of the Kentucky
        Mountaineer Women." Arts and Decoration 41 (May 1934):
        54-5.
        Discusses the work of the American Needlecraft Guild of
Kentucky, noting that quilting never died out in the mountains of
Appalachia. Three black-and-white photos: a quilted tapestry, a
couch cover and a bedspread, with description.

449. "Happy Quilting, Merry Pillow Painting." Redbook 156 (Dec.
        1980): 98-9.
        Photograph of a 42" square that can be decreased or en-
larged. Ideas for making alternative items. Directions for stenciling. Ordering information for diagrams and complete instructions.

450. Hardy, Kay. "Quilt It Yourself." Better Homes & Gardens
        28 (Oct. 1947): 112.
        Directions for using the sewing machine to quilt slip
covers for a chair, head board and waste basket. Discusses special
problems.

451. Harrell, D. Tudor. "Bed Quilt." Hobbies 61 (May 1956):
        37; 45.
        Discusses fabric and technique used in quilts from the
seventeenth century on. Describes quilt patterns from the Colonial
era, the Pioneer period, the Civil War and centennial periods.

452. Harris, Estelle. "Pedigreed Antiques XIX, A Huguenot Heir-
        loom." Antiques 9 (Apr. 1926): 229.
        Black-and-white photo of a chintz appliqué medallion quilt
(9' x 9') that once belonged to Gen. Francis Marion, made by his
mother. Gives a brief history of the family and a description of
the quilt. The fabric is English chintz, with a central tree-and-
birds design.

453. Hartman, Sember. "How to Buy a Quilt." Americana 11
        (March/April 1983): 68-72.
        Discusses the factors that contribute to the quality of a
quilt: fiber content, piecing, appliquéing, quilting, design and color.
Prices vary from region to region. Lists the cost of contemporary
quilts at a shop in New York City. Offers various other prices.
Touches on the "bearding" problem. Gives sample prices for some
styles of pieced quilts reflecting their degree of difficulty. Discusses
how to count the number of quilting stitches per inch and notes that
the number reflects the quality. Suggests traditional color combination for some patterns.

454. "Heirloom Quilts: Bright Accent for Today's Living." Ameri-
        can Home 63 (Nov. 1960): 26-7; 64.

82   QUILTING BIBLIOGRAPHY

Photos of a Baltimore Bride's quilt (1847), an American
Eagle quilt (1800), Star of Bethlehem (1840) and a quilted picture
designed by Florence Peto and dated 1959. Numerous other quilts
pictured. All are from the collection of Mrs. Florence Peto. Interview with Mrs. Peto in which she relates how her collection began.
Article further describes some of the quilts pictured.

455. Hersch, Tandy. "Some Aspects of an 1809 Quilt." Uncover-
      ings 3 (1982): 3-12.
            Black-and-white illustrations. Dissects the construction
of an early quilt by examining the fabric, construction, design and
quilting. Accompanied by footnotes.

456. Hilty, Lucille. "A Passion for Quiltmaking." Uncoverings
      1 (1980): 13-17.
            Essay on the importance of quilting to this author.

457. "Historic Quilts." Antiques 37 (April 1940): 202.
            Book review of Historic Quilts by Florence Peto. Notes
the author's belief that quilts are a reflection of the society that
creates them. Discusses Long Island and Pennslyvania quilts. E. g.,
an Eagle quilt, an autograph quilt and an all-white quilt. Some
examples done by men. Chapter on rare quilts. Author discusses
patterns and their sources. Book has sixty-one plates.

458. Hoag, Norma. "Let's Make a Quilt; with Quilting Designs."
      Design 35 (Dec. 1933): 24-5; 28.
            Discusses construction, fabric, colors, pattern, quilting
frames, linings, quilting designs and finishing. Black-and-white illustrations of quilting designs.

459. _____ . "Quilts, an American Folk Art; Pieced and Appliqué
      with 11 Designs." Design 35 (Mar. 1934): 18-22.
            Photos of Conventional Rose quilt, Democratic Rose, Cake-
stand, Roman Cross, Union Star, Drunkard's Path, Moss Rose, Double Irish Chain, Pine Tree or Weeping Willow. Generally describes
pieced and appliquéd work. Reviews some pattern names: stars,
squares, triangle patterns, crosses and roses.

460. Holstein, Jonathan. "American Quilts as Visual Objects: a
      Personal View." Historic Preservation 24 (Jan. 1972): 28-33.
            Discusses quilts made in America since Colonial times,
patterns, fabric and stuffing. The latter was often dried grass,
leaves, or cotton or wool. Seven quilts photographed in color, four
in black-and-white. Notes the settlers' need for quilts for warmth
and for reasons of thrift. General discussion of their construction
and the evolution of the quilt in America as social circumstances
changed. It was also a way for women to express themselves ar-
tistically. Quilting bees became social institutions.

461. _____ . "Collecting Quilt Data: History from Statistics."
      The Quilt Digest (1983): 62-69.
            Six black-and-white detail photos of quilts. Relates the

evolution of quilts from functional objects to art objects that are studied in films, exhibitions, books and seminars. The author would
like to see these quilts documented with a standard form, recording
construction, fabric, design and size. It is easier to document the
history of a quilt than other forms of folk art because they are less
anonymous. The use of the form would help to determine trends.
Information could then be stored in computers that are being used
more and more by art museums. The author addresses the question
of how to collect, store and retrieve such data. He has devised a
standard questionnaire that could be used with a computer system
and filled out by people who are not textile scholars. Gives sample
pages of the questionnaire.

462. "Homespun Quilt with Hand-Painted Decoration." Antiques 54
      (July 1948): 30.
            Black-and-white frontispiece photo of a quilt from the
collection of Florence Peto. It is sewn in homespun linen thread
decorated by hand-painted blocks and measures nine square feet.
Also shows the reverse of quilt and notes its history.

463. "How to Make Your Own Patchwork Quilts." Redbook 140
      (Mar. 1973): 53-60.
            How to adapt the Log Cabin, Dahlia and Virginia Reel
patterns to smaller items including a child's project using paste on
patchwork. Gives general information on how to choose a design,
fabric and how to figure yardage. Directions for cutting, sewing,
assembling, quilting, and finishing. Black-and-white illustrations of
diagrams for Log Cabin, Virginia Reel and Dahlia. Directions for
smaller items using these patterns: chair seat cover, doll's quilt
and apron.

464. "Instant Heirlooms: Six Country Quilts to Make" Good House-
      keeping 194 (Apr. 1982): 150-3+.
            Four color photos of six quilts from the Phyllis Haders
collection: Delectable Mountains, Grandmothers Flower Garden crib
quilt, North Carolina Lily, Pine Tree, Love Apple Bridal quilt (c.
1850) and Straight Furrow. Mail-order kits for Pine Tree and Grandmothers Flower Garden. Mail-order instructions for Love Apple and
Delectable Mountains. Magazine instructions for North Carolina Lily
and Straight Furrow.

465. James, Michael. "Surviving Without Selling Out: Thoughts
      from a Quilt Artist's Journal." The Quilt Digest (1983): 24-
      29.
            Six color photos of quilts by Michael James: Interweave
I, II, III, IV; The Seasons (1981-1982) and Scene from an Egyptian
Rendezvous with Kites Flying (c. 1982). Artist discusses the dif-
ficulties encountered when trying to maintain artistic freedom in
the marketplace, whether it is a gallery or an agent.

466. Janeiro, Jan. "American Quilts: A Handmade Legacy."
      Fiberarts 8 (July/Aug. 1981): 72.
            Exhibition review of a show at the Oakland Museum that

ran from January 13 to April 1, 1981.   The quilts were exhibited
along with American artifacts with the themes of birth and infancy,
childhood, education, puberty, marriage, family, friendship, community, religion and death.   The show attempted to get the audience
emotionally involved and to appreciate the social role of quilts, and
yet realize that they were made by individual women.   The audience
shares the expressions and feelings of the women of the past through
this exhibit.   One black-and-white photo of a crazy album quilt (1893)
from the museum's collection.

467.   Jarrell, Mary Katherine.   "Three Historic Quilts."   Uncover-
       ings 2 (1981): 97-104.
              Three black-and-white photos of full quilts, with three
detail photos.   Description of quilts in the photos: album quilt, New
York Beauty and Broderie Perse.

468.   Johnstone, Pauline.   "Chinoiserie in English Quilts."   Apollo
       77 (June 1963): 529.
              Essay on examples of Chinese-style embroidery in Eng-
lish quilts in the eighteenth century.   Then they were called sprigged
quilts.   One black-and-white photo of an embroidered satin coverlet
dated 1694, with description.

469.   "Joy of Quilting."   Newsweek 79 (Jan. 10, 1972): 42.
              News item on the quilt revival in cities and in rural areas.
It reflects modern need to conserve.   Reviews rising prices for this
folk art.   Black-and-white photo of Kate and Joel Kopp, owners of
America Hurrah in New York City, with some of their quilts.

470.   Kalter, Suzy.   "Erma Bombeck's Celebrity Quilt."   Ladies'
       Home Journal 99 (Mar. 1982): 79-81; 112.
              One color photo of the entire quilt.   Eight detail photos
of various celebrity blocks: Paul Newman, Johnny Carson and Alan
Alda.   The quilt was autographed by people who have influenced her.
Six tips on how to create an original quilt: use inexpensive materials,
use the personal approach when asking people to contribute, know
that it takes a long time to get the squares returned, ask participants
to write or draw something on the square, provide return postage and
send a thank-you note.

471.   Kile, Michael.   "The Collector: Free Spirit in the West."
       The Quilt Digest (1983): 56-61.
              Six color photos of quilts hanging in the Esprit Building
in San Francisco, where over 200 Amish quilts are displayed for
public viewing.   The author relates the history and description of
the Esprit collection, which began in 1972.   The public can view the
collection by appointment.

472.   Kiracofe, Roderick, comp.   "Showcase."   The Quilt Digest
       (1983): 30-49.
              Color photos of twenty antique and contemporary quilts
with information on quilt name, maker, place, date, size, fabric,
owner and a short statement about the quilt.   E.g., Hearts, by

Jacqueline Eichorn (1982); Tumbling Blocks Variation (c. 1870); Presidents quilt (1852); Forty-Eleven (1982), by Sonya Lee Barrington; Laurel Leaves crib quilt, by Kazi Pietelka (1982); Los Angeles and Vicinity, by Judy Mathieson (1982); Night Rainbow V; The Secondary Bow, by Chris Wolf Edmonds (1982); and a crazy quilt (1893).

473.　Kirkland, Winifred. "Say it with Quilts." Harpers 146 (Jan. 1923): 258-60.
　　　　　　Essay on old quilts and quilting.　Decrys the fact that women no longer speak through needlework but aloud at meetings and in print.　Claims they have lost something in the process.

474.　Klein, Rosemary L. "American Treasury: Quilted Masterpieces." American Home 75 (Oct. 1972): 112-117.
　　　　　　Photos of quilts from the Shelburne Museum.　E.g., New York Beauty, Mariner's Compass, a child's LeMoyne Star (with directions), Star of Bethlehem, Log Cabin, Hexes, Rose of Sharon and others.　Six pages of photos.　Mentions various shapes and pattern names.

475.　Koke, Richard J. "American Quilts." New York Historical Society Quarterly 32 (Apr. 1948): 114-17.
　　　　　　One black-and-white photo of quilts exhibited in the Society's Gallery: a Pin Cushion quilt, Irish Chain, autographed Bridal Quilt, Tulip design crib quilt and others.　Exhibition sponsored by the New York Historical Society.　Quilts are from the society's collection, from the collection of Mrs. Florence Peto and from the Hudson River Museum in Yonkers.　Fifty-two quilts from about 1770 to modern times.　Reviews quiltmaking generally and their use in the New World.　Mentions two autographed quilts in the show.

476.　Koob, Katherine P. "Documenting Quilts by Their Fabrics." Uncoverings 2 (1981): 3-9.
　　　　　　The author has studied American printed fabrics of the late nineteenth century by viewing sample books of fabric.　The article focuses on eleven quilts and attempts to document their fabric.　The emphasis is on the Cocheco Print Works in New Hampshire, the Hamilton Mfg. Co. in Massachusetts and Allens Print Works in Providence, Rhode Island.

477.　Krider, Margaret Young. "Patchwork Quilts." School Arts 56 (Dec. 1956): 13.
　　　　　　Discusses a patchwork quilt project for 4th, 5th and 6th grades.　Choose a story from history, or relate it to geography, natural history, science, a holiday or local industry.　Each child plans a square, chooses his/her materials and cuts the pattern on paper first.　Result: The child sees that all the squares sewn together make a larger unit that tells a story.　One black-and-white photo.

478.　"Ladies Aid Gives Quilt Pageant to Overflow Audience." Life 11 (Sept. 22, 1941): 61-2; 64.
　　　　　　News item on quilt show held in Georges Mills, New

Hampshire.   The women created a play to show their quilts.   The
narrator related the story of each quilt and a performer showed it.
Some of the old quilts were made locally.   E. g., School House quilt,
made after a quilt dated 1825; album quilt (1870); Prairie quilt (1879);
Rolling Star; Fox and Geese; Turkey Tracks and Holly quilt.   Three
black-and-white photos; four color photos, one detail.

479.   Larson, Kay.   "The Craft of Art."   New York   14 (Jan. 1981):
        52-4.
                Exhibition review of Edward Larson's quilts at the Monique
Knowlton Gallery, New York City, held from December 29, 1980 to
January 7, 1981.   Color photo of the Hobo quilt.   Discusses the
fact that worldly objects are now considered art.   Examples from
the show: The Assassination of John F. Kennedy, John Dillinger
quilt, Temptation of the Drive-In, Hobo quilt, George Washington
quilt and Nixon Resignation.

480.   Leach, Mary James.   "Star of the West Quilt."   Antiques   52
        (Nov. 1947):   373.
                News item on a quilt that won first prize in the first
World's Fair held in America in 1853.   It was made by a great-
niece of Henry Clay's wife.   Describes the quilt that is composed
of silk six-pointed stars.

481.   Leman, Bonnie.   "Two Masters: Kretsinger and Stenge."
        Quilter's Newsletter   12 (Jan. 1981):   16-17.
                Description of the quilts illustrated: Paradise Garden,
Orchid Wreath and Iva's Pincushion.   Cover photo: The Quilting
Party quilt, by Bertha Stenge.   Three color photos.

482.   Lindemeyer, Nancy.   "Bright and Bouncy Patchwork Projects."
        Better Homes & Gardens   53 (Oct. 1975):   62-3.
                Color photos of potholders, a vest, tote bag, a child's
smock and a wondow shade.   There are three steps from design to
finished project: paint the designs on muslin, using acrylics; cut
out the design; sew it to the lining; stuff and sew closed.   Directions, and fabric requirements for potholder square and mitt, tote
bag, window shade, child's apron and adult apron.

483.   _____.   "Friendship Quilt: A Beautiful Collection of Shared
        Memories."   Better Homes & Gardens   57 (Feb. 1979):   35-9.
                How the Crafts Department of Better Homes & Gardens
made a friendship quilt for Ciba Vaughan upon her departure from
the staff.   Photo of the finished quilt: thirty twelve-inch squares,
72" x 86".   Directions for making a quilt (p. 176).   Notes the materials, fabric and instructions (pp. 176-180).   Shows directions for
appliqué and cross-stitch and illustrations of nine embroidery stitches.
Gives names of people who made each square.

484.   _____.   "Grandmothers Flower Garden to Quilt as You Go."
        Better Homes & Gardens   55 (April 1977):   104-5.
                The technique involves stitching, stuffing and quilting
each hexagon as it is made.   Instructions with pattern on pp. 168-170.

Shopping information on p. 186. Half-hexagon pattern. Finished
size of quilt is 89" x 109". Notes materials, instructions and diagrams. Two photos.

485.   Lindemeyer, Nancy. "One-Step Quilting for a Classy New
       Look." Better Homes & Gardens 59 (Aug. 1981): 44-7; 50,
       57.
              Color photos of pillows, an apron, a quilt, a tote and a
box. The technique involves tracing the pattern onto muslin, adding
the batt and backing and embroidering with floss. Illustrations of
reduced designs on graphs (or other full-size patterns from the magazine) on p. 168. Gives illustrations of four embroidery stitches and
directions for a quilt (78" x 78"), shown on p. 14.

486.   _____ and Dugan, Deborah. "Quick & Easy Quilting."
       Better Homes & Gardens 58 (Feb. 1980): 160-165+.
              Color photo of an appliquéd quilt based on the Frienship
album quilts. Directions involve stenciling on muslin and then
quilting. Illustration of each block design on graphed squares. Instructions for cutting stencils, preparing fabric, stenciling, quilting
and joining blocks. Ordering information for a stencil kit and fabric
paint.

487.   _____ and Vaughan, Ciba. "Mother Goose Stitch 'n Stuffs
       Nursery Rhyme Dolls & Quilts." Better Homes & Gardens 55
       (Nov. 1970): 130-1.
              Directions for a quilt based on the Mother Goose rhymes.
Shopping information on p. 200 for ordering printed quilt squares.
Reduced drawings of characters sketched on graph paper using a 12"
square. Discusses materials, crayons, fabric markers, appliqué
and beading.
              The method is also applicable to dolls and pillows. In-
cludes one photo.

488.   "Little Known Masterpieces II: Patchwork Quilt." Antiques 1
       (Feb. 1922): 67-68.
              Black-and-white photo of a Rising Sun quilt, from the
South, dated late eighteenth century, no later than 1810. The quilt
measures 12' 6" square and is made of chintz appliqués. It was
dated by an examination of the fabric. It was formerly owned by the
occupant of the old Calvert House in Baltimore. One-page description.

489.   McCrea, Margaret. "Good Ideas From Our Heritage of Quilts."
       Design 44 (Nov. 1942): 8-10.
              Three quilt photos: A Schoolhouse, Pine Tree and Eagle.
Four black-and-white pattern designs and eight quilting designs. The
author laments that the art of quiltmaking is dying out. She gives
ideas for smaller items that take less time: pillows, card table
covers and a jacket. Discusses quilt designs that have been handed
down and mentions The Romance of the Patchwork Quilt in America,
by Hall and Kretsinger and Old Patchwork Quilts and the Women Who
Made Them, by Finley.

490.   Mainardi, Patricia. "Great American Cover-Ups." Art News
        73 (Summer 1974): 30-2.
            Color photos of a Mariner's Compass quilt (c. 1820)
and a Diamond quilt, Amish (c. 1930); black-and-white photo of a
Pineapple quilt (Pa. 1880-1900). The author dates the change in
attitude from quilts as bed covers to quilts as art, to 1971 and
the Whitney Museum exhibit Abstract Design in American Quilts.
Many quilts were not made for use, but for preservation and display
and have never been used. She notes that quilts have a strong design tradition and gives a price range for old quilts. Mentions each
museum that hosted the "Abstract" Show.

491.   _____. "Quilts: The Great American Art." The Feminist
        Art Journal 2 (Winter 1973): 1, 18-23.
            Black-and-white photos: Star Medallion (Philadelphia
1850); a painting by E. W. Perry "The Patchwork Quilt" (1872); Rob-
bing Peter to Pay Paul (nineteenth century, Brooklyn Museum collection); all-white (nineteenth century) and crazy (1875 from the Denver Art Museum). Woman's art has in the past been needlework
that went beyond national boundaries. This is women's "cultural
heritage." It allowed them to express their creativity. Quilts were
not just utilitarian. They were also used for display at home and
at fairs. Women knew they were important work because many
quilts were signed and dated. Quilts were not collective art, but
individual works. African design and Indian culture have influenced
quilt patterns. Design and color were determined by trading and
dying fabric and embroidery. The author discusses categories such
as bridal quilts, presentation quilts, album quilts and memory quilts.
            Discusses how the quilting was done and goes on to say
that women have not been recognized as artists in this field.

492.   Majer, Constance J. "Stay Warm Next Winter: Start a Quilt
        This Spring." Seventeen 40 (Apr. 1981): 65.
            Brief directions for a Nine-Patch quilt, with illustrations.

493.   Malanyn, Margaret. "Fifteen Dearborn Quilts." Uncoverings
        3 (1982): 87-100.
            Article contends that historic events are reflected in
quilts. Uses examples from the Dearborn Museum: Star of Bethlehem, Rose of Sharon and Rocky Road to Kansas. Detailed description of fifteen quilts, interspersed with the maker's family history.
Four black-and-white photos.

494.   Malcom, Janet. "About the House." New Yorker 50 (Sept.
        2, 1974): 68-73.
            Notes the change in attitude toward quiltmaking as work
that elderly ladies did, to its acceptance as modern art. Discusses
The Pieced Quilt: An American Design Tradition, by Jonathan Holstein. Discusses how the pieced quilt fit the need to intersperse
something beautiful into an increasingly mechanistic society, and how
folk art allows the audience to enjoy ornamentation even during trends
of abstractionism. The pieced quilt served this function.

495. _____. "About the House: Exhibition at the Whitney."
New Yorker 47 (Sept. 4, 1971): 60-2.
Exhibition review of the show at the Whitney's Abstract
Design in American Quilts. All the quilts are pieced examples from
the Holstein/van der Hoof collection. They are from New York,
Pennsylvania, New Jersey, Massachusetts, Maine, Vermont and New
Hampshire, and date from the mid-nineteenth century or later. Dis-
cusses the essay by Holstein in the exhibition catalog and the dif-
ference in quality between the antique and contemporary quilts.

496. Mason, Stanley. "The Patchwork Quilt, An American Folk
Art." Graphis 30#172 (1974/75): 126-39 (in English, German and French).
Contains eight color photos and seven black-and-white
photos: Sunshine & Shadow (c. 1870), Log Cabin (c. 1890) and Basket quilt (c. 1830 New England). The photos are from American Quilts
and Coverlets, by Safford and Bishop (1972), and The Pieced Quilt,
by Jonathan Holstein (1973). The author discusses the frugality of
the quiltmakers and the social conditions that made women home-
bound. Relates a short history of quilting bees. Quilts survived
because they were labors of love.

497. Mathieson, Judy. "Some Sources of Design Inspirations for
the Quilt Pattern Mariner's Compass." Uncoverings 2 (1981):
11-18.
Traces the design of the Mariner's Compass pattern from
seventeenth-century sea charts down through early books on quilting
by Ruth Finley and Marie Webster, journal articles by Bonnie Leman
and recent books by Jinny Beyer. Four black-and-white illustrations,
footnotes.

498. "Maysville Quilt." Fiberarts 9 (Sept./Oct. 1982): 100.
Color photo of a Friendship quilt from Maysville, Ga.,
dated 1871, from the collection of the Liberty Corp. of Greenville,
South Carolina.

499. Metzler-Smith, Sandra J. "Quilts in Pomo Culture." Uncoverings 1 (1980): 41-47.
Examines quiltmaking among this group of California Indians noted for their skill in weaving baskets. Accompanied by footnotes.

500. Michelson, Kathy. "Quilting: Patterns of America." Museum
of the Southwest Bulletin (Fall 1981): 4-8; 11.
Article written for the exhibition, History of American
Quilts, held at the Museum of the Southwest, from August 30 to
November 29, 1981. Black-and-white detail photos of Dogwood and
Double Wedding Ring (1916). Color Cover: Wheel of Fortune quilt
(mid-nineteenth century from the Texas Tech. Museum). Black-and-
white photo of Annual #1, 1981, by Nancy Crow. Lists lenders to
the show. Brief bibliography on the history of quiltmaking.

501. "Mixed Motifs in Appliqué." Antiques 41 (June 1942): 354-5.

Black-and-white photo frontispiece.   Appliqué-story-telling quilt
thought to be from Ireland, England or America, eighteenth century,
from the collection of Mrs. W. A. Roden Haworth, New Jersey.
Article describes quilt in detail: a medallion center, appliquéd figures of a late-eighteenth-century Frenchman in military uniform and
animal figures.   Notes materials in the quilt, the color and technique.   History of the families who made and owned the quilt.

502.   Moore, Trevor Wyatt.   "Patchwork Heritage, Appalachia's
        Indigenous Quilting Crafts."   Christian Century 88 (Feb. 17,
        1971):   233.
                Exhibition review of the Mountain Artisans quilt show at
the Rhode Island School of Design.   Briefly reviews the history of
textiles and their import to, and manufacture in New England.   The
designs were imported from England, especially Northumberland,
Devon and Durham Counties.   Discusses the Mountain Artisans, their
environment and their method of producing quilts.   When the work
is done, the quilts are sent to shops nationwide.   The exhibition was
accompanied by forty-four photographs, two films of Appalachia and
tapes of mountain music, all produced by John Cohen.   Two photographs.

503.   "More Great Needlework: Quilted Accessories for Your Home."
        Good Housekeeping 174 (May 1972):   100-1+.
                Two color photos of a coverlet designed by Diantha Field-
ing.   Directions for pillows, Nine-Patch, Five Stripe and Toad in
a Puddle on p. 156.   Ordering information on p. 160 for Posy Bouquet Coverlet, a modern appliqué design (88" x 98").   The kit includes markings for the top.   Directions for pillows include black-
and-white illustrations for color placement and materials needed for
each design.

504.   "Mourning Quilt."   Antiques 26 (July 1934):   36.
                Black-and-white photo of a mourning quilt, submitted by
William R. Dutton of Catonsville, Maryland, accompanied by a description.   Named by its maker, Midnight Star (Aunt Eliza's Star),
measuring 6'10" x 7', it was made before 1896 in black and white.

505.   Murray, Anne Wood.   "The Attitude of the Eagle as Portrayed
        on an Outstanding Group of 'Liberty' Quilts."   Antiques 52
        (July 1947):   28-30.
                Article describes the use of the American Eagle design
on quilts.   The Eagle design can be seen on Oriental export porce-
lain of the late eighteenth century.   The author describes and gives
the history of the quilts shown in the four black-and-white photos:
Eagle quilt (N. Y. 1846), Eagle quilt (Conn. 1793), Delectable Mountains (N. Y. 1810) and a Liberty quilt (Conn. 1790).

506.   Newman, Rachel; Luddede, Jane and Fiore, Louise.   "Quilts
        with Pillow to Match."   American Home 78 (Sept. 1975):
        50-1+.
                Photos of old quilts from the Stearns & Foster quilt col-
lection: Stars of Alabama and Pomegranate.   Page 66 gives directions

for making these quilts. Illustration of full-size pattern pieces and color diagrams. General directions, materials needed and directions for each quilt. Illustration of the finished quilt.

507.   Nickols, Pat. "String Quilts." Uncoverings 3 (1982): 53-57.
        Discusses the construction and design of these quilts.
Footnotes; two black-and-white photos.

508.   "Not So Crazy Quilts." Art News 81 (Mar. 1982): 16-19.
        Exhibition review of The Artist and The Quilt. Eighteen
women artists collaborated with sixteen quilters on a traveling exhibition originated by Charlotte Robinson. A documentary film on
the project is due for public television. Chris Wolf Edmonds made
a quilt based on Alice Neel's painting of her granddaughter. The
quilts are based on work of the artists such as Lynda Benlis and
Alice Baber.

509.   Oldani, John. "Archiving and the American Quilt." Uncover-
        ings 1 (1980): 72-76.
        Describes the Quilt Archive at Southern Illinois University.
Includes a partial listing of quilt patterns held by the archive.

510.   O'Leary, Nora. "To Make for Christmas: A Potpourri of
        Patchwork." Ladies' Home Journal 89 (Nov. 1972): 104-7+.
        Directions for Christmas stocking, patchwork tote, work-
shirt trimmed with appliqué, a necktie, tree hangings, placemat,
pillow, shirt with patchwork yoke and a wraparound skirt. Black-
and-white illustrations, fabric requirements and a color photo of
the finished items.

511.   Oliver, Georgina. "Exhibition American Pieced Quilts at
        Felecity Samuel Gallery London." Connoisseur 184 (Dec. 1973):
        302.
        Exhibition review of show held from December 3, 1973
to January 25, 1974. Compares the pieced quilt to abstract art.
Notes that pattern names reflect life in America and the fabric reflects changes in fashion, economy and spirit. Pieced quilts are
examples of handicraft as a family hobby. Black-and-white photo
of Straight Furrow (1880).

512.   Orr, Ann. "Applique & Trapunto." Better Homes & Gardens
        21 (Feb. 1943): 46-7.
        Part Two of a series started the previous month. Black-
and-white photos of appliqué and stuffed work. General directions
for trapunto and appliqué. Discusses patterns and technique for appliqué.

513.   _____. "Quilt Today--for the Warmth, Fun & Beauty."
        Better Homes & Gardens 21 (Feb. 1943): 44, 56.
        Black-and-white illustrations, and three photos of Star of
Bethlehem, puffy fat quilt and Southern Snowball. Directions for
marking a pattern, putting layers together and quilting.

514. Parker, Julia W. "Commemorative Quilts." <u>Hobbies</u> 59
      (Aug. 1954): 115.
          Author writes about the commemorative quilts she has
made for various American historical events: a World War I Star
quilt in red, white and blue; Lindbergh's flight; Castle Walls in
1936 for Edward VIII; World War I naval quilts; a golden wedding
anniversary quilt; Steps to the White House and the Coronation of
Queen Elizabeth. The author laments the fact that quiltmaking is
becoming a lost art. Hopes people will make quilts to commemorate
the Korean War.

515. "Patch an Heirloom Quilt, with Instructions." <u>Good House-
      keeping</u> 177 (Aug. 1973): 108-9; 168.
          Instructions with diagrams, fabric requirements and di-
rections for cutting and assembling the quilt, including borders and
back. Also gives instructions for pillows. No full-size patterns.
Color photos of pillows and a quilt in the Clay's Choice pattern.

516. "Patchwork Accents to Make for You and Your Home." <u>Good
      Housekeeping</u> 176 (June 1973): 94-5.
          Color photos of a tote bag, kerchief, pillows, potholders
and apron. Includes address for kit to make these items.

517. "Patchwork: As American as Blue Jeans." <u>House and Garden</u>
      139 (Feb. 1971): 68-9; 94.
          Color and black-and-white photos of puff work and a pil-
low designed for the Mountain Artisans by Dorothy Weatherford.
Gives color and fabric ideas. Shopping information and prices on
p. 94. Also notes where to purchase Mountain Artisans' work shown.

518. "Patriotic Quilts (with Portraits of Seven Presidents)." <u>An-
      tiques</u> 35 (June 1939): 304.
          Black-and-white detail photo of a printed cotton quilt
(c. 1830) from the Brooklyn Museum and a photo of the water color
rendering from the <u>Index of American Design</u>. The quilt has like-
nesses of George Washington, John Adams, Thomas Jefferson, John
Madison, James Moore, John Quincy Adams and Andrew Jackson.

519. Patterson, B. M. "Fabric of the Hudson: The River's Story
      as Told by a Quilt." <u>Conservationist</u> 27 (Oct. 1972): 4; 45.
          Two small color photos of a quilt done by the Hudson
River Quilters. Thirty women made the quilt using the Hudson River
as a theme. It was displayed to raise funds for the Hudson River
Conservation projects. This quilt was shown at the Museum of American Folk Art in the exhibition Fabric of the State and in Albany,
Yonkers and Schenectady. In 1969, amateurs and professionals designed a quilt illustrating the beauty of the river. Each woman did
a square showing a different scene along the river.

520. Patterson, Nancy-Lou. "The Traditional Arts of Mennonite
      Women." <u>Artmagazine</u> (Canada) 7 (Dec. 1975): 34-7.
          One color photo; eight black-and-white photos. The author
reviews the work of Mennonite quilters in Ontario, Canada. There

are two branches of the church: Swiss-German, and Dutch-German.
She contrasts their styles based on their folk art heritage.   Photos
show a detail of a Log Cabin, Birds & Plants (1873), appliquéd quilt
with grapes and flowers (c. 1874), apron (1915) and sewing box (1910-
14).

521.   Payant, Felix.   "American Folk Art: Quilts."   Design   39
       (Feb. 1938):   20-1.
            General one-page discussion of quilting: pattern names,
mottoes and appliqué.   Twenty-one black-and-white illustrations of
quilting patterns: fans, shells, diamonds and a feather heart.

522.   Peto, Florence.   "Age of Heirloom Quilts."   Antiques   42
       (July 1942):   32-5.
            Six black-and-white photos: 1.   patches of American
Calico (nineteenth century) from a friendship quilt; 2.   American
cotton print (1889) with pictures of Benjamin Harrison and George
Washington; 3.   an American quilt (nineteenth century) from the Index of American Design; 4.   Simulated patchwork (late nineteenth
century); 5.   cotton patches (late nineteenth century) and 6.   an
American cotton print from the Cranston Print Works, Providence,
Rhode Island.   The author notes that neither condition nor pattern
dictates the age of a quilt.   She writes of the various names of
quilt patterns reflecting politics and migration.   She has studied
binding construction and uses it as a device for dating the quilt.
Dating can also be done by looking at sample fabric books from
earlier eras, design, sets, interlinings and textiles.

523.   _____.   "Birds--Quilted, Patched & Woven."   Antiques   36
       (Nov. 1939):   219; 266-9.
            The editor describes the color cover of toile printed in
pink on white, probably English fabric dated late eighteenth century.
Six black-and-white photos of woven coverlets, whole-cloth quilting
and pieced quilts with birds as a theme on pp. 226-9.   Each plate
is annotated.   The text gives an in-depth description of the photos.
E. g., detail of an Italian quilted bedspread (1864), Freedom quilt
(1840-46), Baltimore Bride's quilt (1851) and a Chintz appliqué (pre-
1800).

524.   _____.   "British Empire in Patchwork."   Antiques   40
       (Sept. 1941):   145.
            One black-and-white photo of an appliquéd medallion quilt
from the collection of Mrs. Barrett Brady.   The author believes
that the quilt commemorates the fiftieth year of the reign of Queen
Victoria.   The textiles (wool, broadcloth, serge and twill) are thought
to be older than the pattern.   The author describes the figures in
the quilt, some of which are animals, harlequins and a ship.

525.   _____.   "Handmade White Elegance."   Antiques   53 (Mar.
       1948):   214-16.
            Six black-and-white photos of all-white stuffed work quilts
from a special exhibit from the author's collection then on view at
the New York Historical Society.   Gives history of this kind of quilt

and the difficulty in its execution.   The author describes certain
common designs and traces their origins.   She discusses the design,
execution and known history of each of the examples in the photographs.

526. _____. "Quilts & Coverlets from New York and Long Island." Antiques 33 (Apr. 1938): 265-267.
          Ten black-and-white photos.   Those quilts illustrated and
annotated in the article were made in or near New York City from
the 1780's to 1853.   The author submits that from looking at these
examples no distinctive technique can be attributed to New York quilts
of this period.   Each photo is accompanied by a description and history.   The owner, maker and materials are noted for Star of Bethlehem, patchwork and appliqué (c. 1810); Chips and Whetstones (prior
to 1828); Wild Goose Chase (early nineteenth century); Grape Vine
and Oak Leaf (nineteenth century) and Presentation quilt (1843).

527. _____. "Textile Discovery." Antiques 61 (Aug. 1953):
120-1.
          Four black-and-white quilt photos.   The J. Hewson factory
was one of the first fabric manufacturing plants established in Philadelphia around 1772.   Includes black-and-white photos of what was
thought to be the only remaining examples of fabric from Hewson's
factory.   The author acquired a spread with fabric similar to the
ones known to be from Hewson's factory.   With the help of the Philadelphia Museum of Art, the author found that the same blocks were
used on her quilt as on the authenticated ones.

528. _____. "Three Generations of Quilts." Antiques 45 (June
1944): 306-7.
          Three black-and-white quilt photos with detailed descrip-
tion: 1.   appliquéd and pieced (late eighteenth century); 2.   Ship's
Wheel pattern (1814) and 3.   Appliquéd quilt (Civil War era).   Notes
the relationship between the design and the era they were made.   Also
notes some family history associated with the quilts.   One photo illustrates a medallion with recurrent borders; one illustrates blocks;
one is similar to an album quilt, but without signatures.

529. "Pictorial Patchwork Quilts." Antiques 25 (May 1934): 169.
          Description of the black-and-white frontispiece photo of
a quilt, dated 1876, depicting a wedding of New England provenance.
The church in the center is surrounded by houses and appliquéd
figures of animals and people.   The quilt is from the collection of
Mrs. Clarence C. Wells of Middlebury, Vt.

530. Platts, Beryl.   "Patchwork Traditions of America." Country
Life (U. K.) 151 (Jan. 6, 1972): 24-5.
          Six black-and-white photos: Harvest Sun, Feathered Star,
Star of Bethlehem and three triangle patterns.   Discusses the begin-
nings of patchwork and appliqué from the ancient Egyptians, the
Crusaders, the Middle Ages and across the ocean to America.   Also
discusses Old Patchwork Quilts, by Ruth Finley (1929) and its 1972

reprinting in England by Bell. Author writes of the subconscious
needs of women to put down roots. Through the evolution of the
pattern, American quiltmakers created a unique folkart. Pattern
names changed with the geography and the social climate of the
times.

531. Pollak, Jane G. "Quilting Bee '75." School Arts 74 (Feb.
      1975): 26-7.
            Each student made one 9" square, using certain specifi-
cations of color, geometric design, trapunto, pieced or appliqué.
The final quilt was 45" x 99". It was auctioned to raise money for
the department. Article accompanied by seven black-and-white photos.

532. "Punch Patchwork Easy, Colorful and Fun to Sew." Better
      Homes & Gardens 51 (Nov. 1973): 86-7; 136; 150.
            Color photos of patchwork quilts created by Ciba Vaughan:
One-patch quilts on a bed, a quilted pillow sham, Star pattern as a
pillow and a curtain. Includes sewing directions, fabric requirements and directions and where to order kits for the pillow sham.

533. "Q is for Quilts to Appliqué." Good Housekeeping 188 (May
      1979): 168; 226; 196.
            Color photos of two children's quilts: Farm Friends--
six blocks, 44" x 60", order coupon for pattern on p. 226 and Mr.
Rabbit and the Carrot Patch quilt--directions and fabric requirements
and quilting diagram. No full-size pattern.

534. "Quilt from Ohio." Antiques 58 (Dec. 1950): 501.
            News item from a subscriber of the magazine mentioning
a family quilt made of linen and muslin (c. 1816). The technique
is raised and padded work. One black-and-white photo.

535. "Quilt Postscripts." Antiques 57 (May 1950): 379.
            News item on Baltimore Presentation quilts. One bears
the name of General Z. Taylor. The other also is inscribed as
being presented to Zachary Taylor in 1847. Three black-and-white
photos.

536. "Quilted Bonds." Antiques 42 (July 1942): 35.
            One black-and-white photo of a quilted appliquéd bedspread.
The design was copied from a quilt of the Civil War era brought
home by a Union soldier. The original was patchwork, the new one,
appliquéd. It is owned by the maker's daughter, Mrs. June Martin
of Fowler, Ohio.

537. "Quilting." House and Garden 123 (March 1963): 140-3.
            Twelve color illustrations of quilt blocks with designs
such as, a Pear section, Acorn, Spider Web and Shells. Color
photos of three quilts: appliquéd Anemones, patchwork Squares and
quilted Mushrooms, all designed by House and Garden. Includes
ordering information for patterns and directions and ideas for making your own.

538. "Quilting Party with Recipes." Seventeen 31 (Dec. 1972): 116-119+.
        Proffers the idea of quiltmaking at a party, giving each guest a square. Color photo of the finished quilt and the address for appliqué patterns and instructions. Black-and-white diagrams for cutting.

539. "Quiltmaking, the Modern Approach to a Traditional Craft, by Ann Sargent-Wooster." Book review. American Artist 38 (April 1974): 10-13.
        The book has 270 illustrations, eighty-four black-and-white photos, twenty-four color photos, diagrams, a dictionary and a bibliography. The review discusses Being at the Forest Entrance, by Nell B. Sonneman; Box Pod quilt, by Bonnie Gisel; and the Hudson River quilt.

540. "Quilts & Coverlets: Homespuns of the Northwest Territory." Antiques 87 (Mar. 1965): 327-9.
        Eight black-and-white photos, including one quilt (1814) with a detail photo, signed, and a verse sampler (1850), appliquéd. Article written in conjunction with the issue on the Northwest Territory.

541. "Quilts as Art (Exhibition of work of Mrs. B. Stenge)." Newsweek 22 (Aug. 2, 1943): 91.
        News item on the quilt show at the Art Institute of Chicago. Seventeen quilts made over the past thirteen years by Bertha Stenge. They are said to be "the finest modern quilts in the United States today." All the designs are original and all are double-bed size.

542. "Quilts as Art." Antiques 100 (Aug. 1971): 162; 166.
        Exhibition review of Abstract Design in American Quilts at the Whitney, a show of about 60 quilts out of a collection of 200, made between 1820 and 1930. They were chosen for their visual impact and indicate the innate sense of artistry of the quiltmakers. The quilts are a record of the textiles used in certain fashion periods.

543. "Quilts: Baby and Doll Quilts." New Yorker 52 (Dec. 6, 1976): 40-1.
        In the Talk of the Town column. Quilt exhibition review-- A Child's Comfort: Baby and Doll Quilts in American Folk Art at the Museum of American Folk Art. Sixty-four quilts made between 1830 and 1976 from Pennsylvania, New York and New England. Reviews the construction of crib quilts.

544. "Quilts from Hawaii." Newsweek 12 (Dec. 5, 1938): 23.
        Exhibition review of the first big show of Hawaiian folk art in the United States at the Folk Arts Center in New York City. Items are from the Honolulu Academy of Arts and its show in September. Twenty-six quilts made between 1825 and 1938. The show includes a Samoan quilt given to Robert Louis Stevenson in 1890.

545. "Quilts with Schoolhouse, American Eagle, Democratic Rose,
and Cake Stand Design." Design 36 (Dec. 1934): 42-6.
Photos of Little Red School House (1865-70), American
Eagle (1855), Democratic Rose and Cake Stand quilts. General essay
on various block names and a brief description of quilt construction;
variations on the square, triangle, cross, mottoes on quilts, stars,
and appliqué patterns, flowers and leaves.

546. Ramsey, Bets. "Design Invention in Country Quilts of Tennessee and Georgia." Uncoverings 1 (1980): 48-55.
Seeks to define quilts made in the rural South. The author believes that availability of fabric affects the design. Footnotes.
Three black-and-white photos.

547. Reals, Lucille F. "Antique American Quilts." Hobbies 65
(Dec. 1960): 28-9.
Cover illustrates several quilts selected by the author
as examples of nineteenth-century workmanship from women of that
era. They represent thrift, the use of leisure time, romance, love
of nature, scriptural influences and patriotism. Gives brief descriptions of some of the quilts on the cover: LeMoyne Star, Turkey
Tracks and album quilts.

548. Reddall, Winifred. "Pieced Lettering on Seven Quilts Dating
from 1833-1891." Uncoverings 1 (1980): 56-63.
Comparison of quilts pieced so as to inscribe a message.
Notes the unique message and style of the Vosburgh quilt, dated 1874.
Black-and-white illustrations.

549. Robertson, Elizabeth Wells. "Modern Quilts." Design 36
(Jan. 1935): 8-13; 26.
Photos of quilts made by Elizabeth Robertson. Essay on
the Colonial history of the United States and the need for quilts.
Notes crazy quilts, Brick work and the history of quilt names. Some
are taken from nature, such as flowers and stars, some have reli-
gious names. Describes quilt construction. Notes the exhibitions
where her quilts have been shown, both in the United States and England. Quilts illustrated: Caprice, Birds of the Jungle and Tree of
Life.

550. "Romance of the Patchwork Quilt in America." Antiques 31
(Jan. 1937): 42.
Book review of the Hall/Kretsinger book. Notes Carrie
Hall's block collection of over 1,000 items on display at the Thayer
Museum at the University of Kansas. Lauds the illustrations of 700
patches and 119 plates of whole quilts made from the seventeenth to
the twentieth centuries. The book is a catalog of quilt patterns.
Gives the book a generally good review because it filled a long-felt
need.

551. Rosson, Lea. "Quilts at the University of Kansas Museum of
Art." Antiques 104 (Dec. 1973): 1102-5.
Nine black-and-white photos, including an appliquéd and

pieced medallion quilt from Bucks Co., Pa. (1848). Illustration
from Univ. of Kansas Museum of Art (William B. Thayer Memorial
Collection and Malcom James Collection), with description. Chips
and Whetstones (Ky. 1850); Pineapple & Church Steps (1900) and
Orchid Wreath, by Rose Kretsinger. Notes the maker, if known.

552.   Rowley, Nancy J.   "Red Cross Quilts for the Great War."
       Uncoverings 3 (1982):   43-51.
            Discusses quiltmaking to raise money for the Red Cross
during World War I.   Describes some autograph quilts made during
those years.   Footnotes, bibliography and three black-and-white
photos.

553.   Saffer, Sandra C.   "America's Quilts & Coverlets, by Carl-
       ton Safford and Robert Bishop."   Antiques 103 (June 1973):
       1110.
            Book review is critical of some of the technical informa-
tion.   Excellent illustrations, unreliable captions.   Two inaccurate
descriptions of coverlets and a misprint.   Positive comment: the
book brings to public's attention many unpublished examples of pieced
and appliquéd work.

554.   Schwartz, Marvin D.   "Antiques: Wide Variety in Early
       Quilts."   New York Times 5 (Feb. 1972):   26.
            Quilts from the eighteenth and nineteenth centuries were
whole cloth, linsey-woolsey, linen without wool and Indian painted
cottons.   One may surmise from the whole cloth what fabrics were
used in eighteenth- and nineteenth-century bedrooms.

555.   "Sew Up a Quick Quilt: A Nifty Way to Recycle an Old
       Blanket."   Seventeen 36 (Nov. 1977):   42.
            Brief directions for making a quilt from patterned sheets
and a blanket using the sewing machine.   Black-and-white illustrations.

556.   "Sew Your Own Magazine Cover Quilt."   Saturday Evening Post
       250 (Jan. 1978):   22-5.
            Idea based on Chris Edmonds' George Washington Quilt,
done in 1976 from a Saturday Evening Post painting of Washington.
The magazine asked Ms. Edmonds to make a quilt from a Norman
Rockwell cover.   She chose "The Little Spooners," a painting done
in 1926.   Article includes directions for making this quilt.   Color
photo of Edmonds' Little Spooners quilt and her George Washington
quilt.   Directions for buying the fabric, cutting, enlarging the draw-
ing (p. 25), transferring the picture to cloth and finishing the quilt.
Also gives full-size patterns for the pieced border of the Little Spooners quilt.

557.   Shapiro, David.   "American Quilts."   Craft Horizon 31 (Dec.
       1971):   42-45; 72.
            Exhibition review: Abstract Design in American Quilts
at the Whitney, July 1 to October 5, 1971.   Three black-and-white
photos; one color.   E.g., Rainbow Stripes (Pa. c. 1860), Kaleidoscope (Pa. c. 1860), crazy (Pa. c. 1850) and Log Cabin (Pa. 1850).

558. "Shem, Ham et al. on a Quilt." Antiques 70 (Dec. 1956): 574.

    "Collector's notes": black-and-white photo and description of a Noah's Ark quilt made by the owner's great-grandmother who lived from 1818 to 1872. From the collection of Duncan Groner.

559. Sherrill, Sarah B. "Exhibition review Amish Quilts: The Mint Museum of Art." Antiques 110 (Sept. 1976): 462.

    Exhibition of Amish quilts from the collection of Phyllis Haders. Fourteen from Pennsylvania, Indiana and Ohio made between 1850 and 1935. Twelve full-size, one cradle and one trundle quilt.

560. _____ . "Folk Design in American Quilts." Antiques 105 (Apr. 1974): 686.

    Exhibition review of show at the Newark Museum, which also presented one of the first shows of quilts as a form of popular art in 1948. The museum's collection now has over 125 pieced and appliquéd quilts. Between 30 and 40 quilts acquired since 1948 are in the current show organized by Phillip H. Curtis, curator of Decorative Arts. Examples are from mid-eighteenth century to the early twentieth century. Most were made or used in New Jersey. Black-and-white photo: Tulips in a Vase (c. 1852), with a history of the maker and the quilt.

561. _____ . "Hawaiian Quilts." Antiques 116 (July 1979): 68-70.

    Exhibition review of show at the Museum of American Folk Art, New York City, from July 3 to Sept. 2, 1979. It was a show of twenty-five Hawaiian quilts dating from the early nineteenth century through the early twentieth century. They were from private collections, the Honolulu Academy of Arts and the Bernice P. Bishop Museum in Honolulu. The article relates the history of Hawaiian quilting. The patterns resemble designs carved into wood and printed on tapa. Hawaiian quilts are individual artistic expressions and the patterns are the exclusive property of the designer, who believed her soul was incorporated into the craft. To steal or borrow a pattern was to rob that woman of her identity. Black-and-white illustration of Crowns and Scepters (1886).

562. _____ . "Quilts & Coverlets." Antiques 118 (Aug. 1980): 192.

    Exhibition review of show at the St. Louis Art Museum held from August 14 to October 12, 1980, entitled Take Cover! Quilts & Coverlets from the St. Louis Art Museum Collection. The show included American pieced, appliquéd and embroidered quilts. There were examples of fabric block printed in Philadelphia by John Hewson, a Baltimore Friendship quilt and white work with candlewick embroidery (1821). There was an example of a Friendship quilt signed and dated 1848 and a cotton bedspread block printed by John Hewson with trapunto and quilting (1809).

563. _____ . "Quilts and Coverlets in Denver." Antiques 106 (July 1974): 25; 28.

Review of the first exhibition of the Denver Art Museum
quilt collection of over 200 quilts shown in its entirety. Examples
from the eighteenth, nineteenth and twentieth centuries. There were
American, English and Hawaiian examples from the Honolulu Academy
of Arts and some from private collectors. Quilt styles were pieced,
appliquéd and crazy. Detail photo of an appliquéd quilt (1863) by
Elizabeth Ann Cline.

564. _____. "Quilts at the Metropolitan Museum." Antiques
       106 (July 1974): 28, 32.
              Exhibition review of eleven quilts and one coverlet from
the Metropolitan Museum of Art's American Wing. Many were acquired in the past two years and were chosen for their aesthetic
qualities. The show represents many patterns and techniques, both
appliquéd and pieced. Black-and-white photo of Star of Bethlehem
(1834-45) with description.

565. _____. "Quilts (Baltimore Album Quilts)." Antiques 118
       (Nov. 1980): 856; 860.
              Black-and-white photo of a Baltimore Album quilt (1852)
made for Isabella Battee. Exhibition review of a show held from
November 18, 1980 to January 11, 1981 at the Museum of Fine Arts,
Houston, Texas. It traveled to the Metropolitan Museum of Art in
New York City and the Baltimore Museum of Art. Between sixteen
and twenty-five quilts were shown at each museum. About one-half
of them were from the Baltimore Museum of Art, some were from
other museums and private collections. The author notes the history of album quilts. The show was organized by Dena Katzenburg.

566. _____. "Quilts in Kansas: The Helen Foresman Spencer
       Museum of Art at the University of Kansas, Lawrence." An-
       tiques 113 (July 1978): 1222; 1224.
              Exhibition review of show held from June 18 to July 30,
1978. The quilts were displayed in the Kress Gallery, and in the
Watkins Community Museum, downtown. More were on display during the Kansas Quilt Symposium held from July 20 through 22 in the
Kress Gallery, the Central Court of the Spencer Museum and in the
Student Union. The collection was started by Sallie Casey Thayer
in the early part of the twentieth century. The museum now owns
more than 150 quilts. Black-and-white photo of a One-Patch (c. 1880),
with description.

567. _____. "Quilts: Old Courthouse, Lancaster, Pa." An-
       tiques 114 (July 1978): 48; 52.
              Exhibition review of a show held from July 16 to 29,
1978. Forty quilts made in Lancaster County, Pa. over the past
150 years. The show was entitled Quilts in the Garden Spot, and
was part of Lancaster Summer Arts Fest. Some of the quilts were
family heirlooms that have always remained in this locale. There
were some Amish quilts from private collections and the Pennsylvania Farm Museum of Landis Valley. E.g., a Red Tulip (1815)
and Oakleaf (1849).

568. _____. "Southern Comfort: Quilts from the Atlanta Historical Society Collection." Antiques 113 (June 1978): 1224;
1228.
           Exhibition review of show held from June 4 to October
7, 1978. It featured sixteen nineteenth-century quilts, many never
exhibited before. The author notes that the show is a valuable con-
tribution to the study of American textile art, expecially that of the
southeast. All the quilts were made in Georgia or owned by Geor-
gians. They span almost the entire nineteenth century, illustrating
many patterns and techniques.

569. _____. "White-Work Bed Coverings Exhibition at the DAR
Museum." Antiques 114 (Aug. 1978): 194; 198.
           Examples of white-work bed coverings made in America
between 1800 and 1840, using techniques such as Marseilles quilting,
candlewicking and flat embroidery. It was a show of twenty quilts,
most with a large central motif. Black-and-white photo: white-on-
white candlewick (1827). Author explains the technique and its history. She also discusses candlewicking, contrasting machine and
hand examples. She gives other examples of flat embroidery stitches.

570. "Short Cuts for Quilters." Better Homes & Gardens 41 (Jan.
1963): 80-2.
           Four color photos of a quilt, vanity stool, waste basket,
quilted panels on a screen and swing cushion, all quilted. Designed
by Jean Ray Laury. General directions for measuring, mixing colors
and pressing.

571. Silber, Julie. "The Reiter Quilt: A Family Story in Cloth."
The Quilt Digest (1983): 50-55.
           Six color photos of the quilt, five detail and two black-
and-white photos of the Reiter family. Relates the story of an album
quilt shown to the author in her shop. Traces the family history of
the quilt's maker from the Austro-Hungarian Empire to Pennsylvania.
Connects its style to German influences in Newark, N. J. and Mc-
Keesport, Pa. The craft of quilting was not done in Eastern Europe.
Tries to relate some of the symbols on the quilt to the experiences
of the two makers, relying on what is known of their ancestry.

572. "Sophisticated Quilts." Art Digest 20 (Sept. 1946): 12.
           Exhibition review of a show at the Bertha Schaefer Gal-
lery. Over twelve quilts made by Ethel Bean, with price range.
Reviewer calls them "pictures in modern idiom."

573. Springer, L. E. "A Baltimore Friendship Quilt." St. Louis
Art Museum Bulletin 9 (May/June 1973): 1-3.
           Describes a Baltimore Friendship quilt made in 1848:
twenty-five squares, many with signatures. Notes its color and
composition. Its complete history is not known. Author believes
it is one of the finest examples of its type. Black-and-white photo.
Black-and-white detail photo on the cover.

574. "Star of Bethlehem." Design for Arts in Education 82 (Sept.
1981): cover.

Color cover: Star of Bethlehem quilt from the Index of
American Design, National Gallery of Art, Washington, D. C.

575. "Stars and Feathers. " Antiques 35 (Jan. 1940): 15.
            One black-and-white photo of a Union quilt (c. 1861) from
Franklin County, Pennsylvania, owned by Mrs. Charles Knepper.
The quilt has an American Eagle appliqué, a design that dates from
the Civil War. It was made by Mrs. Charles Bork. A descriptive
article accompanies the photograph obtained from Mrs. Florence
Peto.

576. Stillman, Marjorie. "It's a Child's World Quilt. " Creative
        Crafts 6 (Aug. 1979): 40-3.
            One color photo, eleven black-and-white photos, and a
color cover of the quilt. It comprises thirty blocks of a child's
artwork transferred to fabric, using embroidery for emphasis. The
author gives directions and materials needed for a 72" x 86" quilt.
She recommends tracing paper to draw patterns of the figures, with
a 1/4" seam allowance, then pinning shapes to (15") blocks and appliquéing them.

577. "Stitch in Another Time. " Time 86 (Aug. 6, 1965): 60-1.
            Two color photos: a crazy quilt from the Newark Museum
Show and a view of the gallery showing both Princess Feather and
Rising Star quilts. The great era in quiltmaking was from 1750 to
1870. Talks about pattern names, their history, their uses and the
difficulty in obtaining fabric.

578. "Story Book Quilts. " Art Digest 20 (Dec. 15, 1945): 8.
            Exhibition review of a show of the same name. Quilts
done by Marion Cheever Whiteside are likened to tapestry. The
cutout figures are set off by background colors. E. g. , Mother
Goose theme, Helen of Troy series, Queen of Heart's series. Loaned
by museums or private collectors.

579. Sunderline, Sylvia. "Address Book: Quilt Stores. " House
        Beautiful 119 (Jan. 1977): 18.
            Lists addresses for many dealers, noting inventory (in-
cluding dates, number of quilts, price range and condition). E. g. ,
America Hurrah Antiques, Laura Copenhaven Industries, Craft House,
Cora Ginsburg, Barbara Janos and Barbara Ross, Paul Lewis and
many more.

580. Tanner, Laura. "If You Want It to Look Luxurious Quilt It. "
        House Beautiful 96 (June 1954): 104-7.
            Color and black-and-white photos of quilted furniture up-
holstery, beds and chairs. Ideas for custom quilting, including pur-
chasing prequilted fabric, using fabric that copies patterns on old
quilts and using fabric with a built-in pucker.

581. Taylor, Nick. "Old Kentucky Quilts. " Americana 10 (Jan./
        Feb. 1983): 46-50.
            Article on the Kentucky Quilt Project. The author relates

how the old quilts were prepared for the show and how the quilt
histories were obtained. He notes that the quilts will become part
of the Smithsonian Institution Traveling Exhibition Service. Six color
photos, one black-and-white photo and a color cover.

582. "Tender Loving Care for Antique Quilts." Better Homes &
    Gardens 54 (Oct. 1976): 52-56.
        Discusses identifying quilt fabrics, cleaning woolen and
cotton quilts, machine washing, removing stains, mending, storing,
and displaying.

583. Terrace, Lisa C. "Appliqué Quilt." Bulletin, Museum of
    Fine Arts Boston 62 (1964): 162-63.
        Black-and-white photo and essay on the Harriet Powers
quilt, made between 1895 and 1898. Gives its history, color placement and describes several of the blocks.

584. "Toss off a Summer Quilt." Decorating Craft Ideas 14 (Aug.
    1983): 68.
        Idea for making a quilt using two sheets, a light thermal
blanket and tying the quilt with ribbon. Includes shopping information and addresses.

585. Toth, Cecelia K. "Quilts for Now & From Long Ago." Good
    Housekeeping 184 (April 1977): 110-13+.
        Four pages of color photos of quilts from the Thomas K.
Woodard collection: 1. Bow Tie quilt (1890); 2. Basket quilt (late
nineteenth century); 3. Schoolhouse quilt (c. 1910) and 4. Clipper
Ship quilt. Page 114 announces and gives rules for Good Housekeeping's Great Quilt Contest. Directions for cutting, assembling
and buying fabric for nos. 1-3. Number four can be made from a
kit. Two black-and-white sketches.

586. "Tour de Force in Printed Cotton." Antiques 71 (June 1957):
    560-1.
        Four black-and-white photos of a pictorial quilt gift to
the Farmer's Museum at Cooperstown, N. Y. Includes a description of the fabric, the dye and a detail of the quilt sewn by the
donor's great-great-grandmother.

587. "Treasury of Amish Quilts to Make for Your Own Home."
    Good Housekeeping 190 (Mar. 1980): 128-33.
        Five pages of color photos of quilts from the collection
of Phyllis Haders, with instructions: 1. Sunshine and Shadow;
2. Double Nine-Patch; 3. Bars (1890); 4. Center Diamond (1920)
and 5. Double Wedding Ring from the collection of Thomas K.
Woodard. Page 258 notes where to order directions for making
Amish quilts.

588. "Tulip and Star Quilt." Hobbies 60 (Mar. 1965): 45.
        Cover illustration described on page 45. Recently auc-
tioned for $140 by Parke-Bernet Galleries Inc.

589. Tuska, Miriam. "Kentucky Quilts." Antiques 105 (Apr.
      1974):   784-90.
          Fifteen black-and-white and color photos of Kentucky
quilts, giving the artist's name, technique, colors, history, size
and place where it is housed. E. g., 1. Star of Lemoyne (1839),
with detail; 2. Blazing Sun (early nineteenth century), with detail;
3. Star of Bethlehem (nineteenth century); 4. crazy (late Victorian);
5. Four-Pointed Star Pattern (Victorian); 6. Appliqué from the Kentucky Historical Society; 7. quilt embroidered with crewel and candlewick; 8. Barn Raising (1910) and 9. Mosaic Star (early 1860's).

590. Vaughan, Ciba. "Crayon Quilt." Better Homes & Gardens
      53 (Jan. 1975):   58-9.
          Idea for preserving children's artwork on a quilt. In-
structions for transferring crayon drawings from paper to fabric.
Examples show alternate squares of art and solid fabric using a 13"
square. The finished quilt is 66" x 90". Shopping information on
p. 80. Page 44 notes materials needed, step-by-step directions
and sizes for various beds. Four photos.

591. Walker, Alexandra. "Paint a Quick Quilt." American Home
      75 (Jan. 1972):   58-9; 75.
          Directions for painting a quilt by drawing lines on a sheet
and painting in the spaces. Gives materials needed and sewing directions. Black-and-white photos.

592. Walker, Ragnhild T. "Quilted Cuties." Better Homes & Gar-
      dens 21 (April 1943):   67.
          Idea for small novelty items. Notes where to write for
transfer designs and directions. One black-and-white photo.

593. Weissman, Judith R. "Quilts of Baltimore." Americana 9
      (Jan. /Feb. 1982):   24-8.
          Describes the derivation of the Baltimore Album quilt.
Most date from 1843 to 1852. Twenty-four of these quilts are on
display at the Baltimore Museum of Art. The exhibition sought to
discover whether they were the work of many sewers or only a few.
Dena Katzenburg answered that question through three years of research. Relates the detective work involved in documenting these
quilts. Three color photos; two black-and-white photos.

594. "West Virginia Women Find Cash in Quilts with Aid of VISTA
      Man." Aging 198 (Apr. 1971):   14.
          News item about West Virginia women selling their quilts
through Cabin Creek Quilts, a cooperative organized by a Vista
worker. The quilts are in stores around the country.

595. Westbrook, Nicholas and Gilman, Carolyn. "Minnesota Patch-
      work." Minnesota History 46 #6 (Summer 1979):   237-245.
          Five black-and-white, and eight color photos of quilts
from the show Minnesota Patchwork including a crazy, Lone Star
and Five-Patch, with footnotes. The quilts are from the collection
of the Minnesota Historical Society. The article reviews the exhibit

of thirty-five quilts from the society's collection of over 120 quilts, selected on the basis of quality of workmanship, design and condition. The society's collection is not representative of Minnesota society at that time, it represents only those well-to-do families who donated quilts to the museum. The society's quilts do document the techniques and materials used beginning in the late eighteenth century.

596. Whittemore, Margaret. "Doctor Syntax Quilt: Great Grand-
      father's Comic Strip." Antiques 55 (Mar. 1949): 182-3.
            The article describes a quilt used by the author's grand-
      father. The theme and pictures are based on a character developed
      by Thomas Rowlandson (1756-1827). Comic views of English life.
      Five black-and-white photos.

597. Yost, Mrs. Harry. "Quilt Story." Hobbies 58 (Oct. 1953):
      43; 60.
            Relates the story of the author's mother, who began piec-
      ing quilts in 1887 in Nebraska. Discusses growing up on the prairie
      in those years. The quilts her mother made include a Lone Star,
      Wild Goose Chase, Necktie and Post Card. Quilts by the author's
      mother were exhibited in New York City in 1952, at the Women's
      International Exposition.

598. American Quilt Designs.
       Eighty slides with lecture script and bibliography. Rental
       only. Center for the History of American Needlework,
       Carlow College, 3333 Fifth Ave., Pittsburgh, Pa. 15213.

599. American Quilts: A Handmade Legacy.
       Slide/lecture by Julie Silber. 280 slides from the show of
       the same name held in 1981, illuminated with personal re-
       search in the exhibits. Available: 2838 Atwell Ave., Oak-
       land, Calif. 94601.

600. American Quilts, Granny's Quilts.
       Film, 15 min., color, sound, 1974, 16mm. An elderly
       woman talks about quilting: the stitches and fabric used in
       making patchwork and appliqué. Distributor: Highlights
       Productions, Dale Zalen 24220 112th Ave., Maple Ridge,
       B. C. V2X 7E6, Can.

601. Amish Quilts.
       Forty slides (#48). Ontario Crafts Council. Historic quilts
       from the Canadian Amish. Crafts Resource Centre, 346
       Dundas St. West, Toronto, M5T 1G5, Can. *

602. Anonymous Was a Woman.
       Film, 28 min., color, sound. Produced and directed by
       Mirra Bank. Illustrates eighteenth- and nineteenth-century
       woman's folk art in America. Narrated from sources of
       that day. Distributor: Films Inc., 733 Green Bay Rd.,
       Wilmette, Ill. 60091.

603. Antique Quilts of New Hampshire.
       Slides, 1976. Oldest quilts in the state, accompanied by
       script, history and pattern identification. Available from
       Jane W. Winge, Clothing and Textiles Specialist, Coopera-
       tive Extension Service, North Dakota State University, Fargo,
       N. D. 58102.

---

*Due to Customs regulations, slides from the Ontario Crafts Council
are not available outside of Canada.

604.   Art Americana: Quilts and Coverlets.
        Sixty-one slides.   Slides of the 1975 Rochester Institute of
        Technology exhibition of quilts from private collections.
        Available: Your Portable Museum, American Craft Council,
        44 West 53rd St., New York, N. Y.   10019.   Also from
        Ontario Crafts Council, Crafts Resource Centre, 346 Dun-
        das St., Toronto, Ont.   M5T 1G5, Can.

605.   Art for Use.
        Quilt slides, 34mm color with printed descriptive notes.
        American Crafts Council exhibit commissioned by the Na-
        tional Fine Arts Commission for the 13th Winter Olympic
        Games 1980.   American Crafts Council, 44 West 53rd St.,
        New York, N. Y.   10019.

606.   Beds, Sweet Dreams & Other Things.
        Sixty slides (#143).   Quilts and wall hangings, soft sculp-
        ture and clothing from the Surface Design Exhibition 1979.
        From: Ontario Crafts Council, Crafts Resource Centre,
        346 Dundas St. West, Toronto, Ont.   M5T 1G5, Can.

607.   Before the Industrial Revolution.
        Film, 17 min., color, sound, 1974.   Shows old-time crafts
        including quilting.   Distributor: Vedo Films, 85 Longview
        Rd., Port Washington, N. Y.   10050.   Produced and di-
        rected by Vincent Tortora.

608.   Born Under a Log Cabin.
        Film, 9-1/2 min., color, sound.   Meeting with a woman
        who has made many quilts by hand.   Distributor: Thomas
        W. Peck, Filmedit, 229 Crowley Ave., Lansing, Mich.
        48823.   Directed and produced by Thomas W. Peck.

609.   Contemporary Quilters in and Around Toronto.
        116 slides, 1980.   Work by artists such as Laurie Swim,
        Margaret S. Colle and Susan MacDonald.   Also shows de-
        tails of an antique crazy quilt.   Available: Ontario Crafts
        Council, 346 Dundas St. West, Toronto, Ont.   M5T 1G5,
        Can.

610.   Contemporary Quilting and Appliqué.
        Twenty-six slides.   Slides show modern quilting in banners,
        coverlets and clothing.   Available: Ontario Crafts Council,
        346 Dundas St. W., Toronto, Ont.   M5T 1G5, Can.

611.   Festival of the West 1977.
        134 slides and cassette.   Available from: Clothing Special-
        ist, Utah State University, Cooperative Extension Service,
        Family Life, 207 UMC 29, Logan, Utah   84322.   Illustrates
        quilts from the show of the same name.   Accompanied by
        catalog illustrating black-and-white photos of quilts annotated
        with quilt history.   59pp.

612. Four Women Artists.
      Film, 25 min., color, 16mm, sound, 1978. Interview with
      four women artists from Mississippi, including a quilter.
      They discuss their motivation as artists. Distributor: Cen-
      ter for Southern Folklore, 1216 Peabody Ave., Box 4081,
      Memphis, Tenn. 38104.

613. Hale, Roy. Quilt Slides.
      Color, 35mm. Features whole quilts and detail slides of
      pieced and appliquéd work in traditional, contemporary,
      novelty and antique patterns, e.g., Dresden Plate, Ohio
      Rose, Japanese Playing Cards, Milky Way and Rose of
      Sharon. Produced by Roy L. Hale, 2445 21st Ave., San
      Francisco, Calif. 94116.

614. The Hardman Quilt: Portrait of an Age.
      Film, 10 min., color, sound, 16mm, 1975. Shows the ap-
      pliqué work in the Hardman quilt, emphasizing its texture
      and color. Suggests that it illustrates the life of its maker.
      Distributor: Lawren Productions, 12121 Pinewood, Box 666,
      Mendocino, Calif. 95460. Director/Producer: Hans Hal-
      berstadt.

615. Harriet Powers Pictorial Quilt.
      Slide set with details of the Harriet Powers quilt. Available:
      Slide Library, Museum of Fine Arts--Boston, 465 Huntington
      Ave., Boston, Mass. 02115.

616. Kaleidoscope.
      Film, 3 min., color, sound, 1978. Shows patchwork quilt
      designs as though in a kaleidoscope. No narration. Dis-
      tributor: Darino Films, Box 5173, New York, N. Y.
      10017. Director/Producer Eduardo Darino.

617. Kathleen Ware, Quiltmaker.
      Film, 33 min., color, sound, 16mm, 1979. Focuses on
      making a Lone Star quilt from beginning to end, including
      glimpses into the artist's daily life. Distributor: Folklore
      Program, English Dept., University of Oregon, Eugene,
      Ore. 97403. Made by Sharon Sherman, Eugene, Ore.

618. Lap Quilting.
      Public Television series--twelve 30 min. programs. Georgia
      Bonesteel, Creator, Hendersonville, North Carolina. Pro-
      ducer: University of North Carolina, UNC-TV Network, 202
      University Square West, Chapel Hill, N. C. 27514. Dis-
      tributed through Southern Educational Communications Assn.
      Now includes thirteen new episodes in addition to the twelve
      original parts of the series. Part Two discusses fabric and
      quilt design, how to execute advanced patterns and how to
      finish a quilt. There are two programs on quilted clothing.

619. Looking at Quilts.

Slide/tape lecture, sixty-three slides, by Scott Robson, cu-
rator Historic Bldgs. and Furnishing, Nova Scotia Museum,
Education Loans, 1747 Summer Street, Halifax, Nova Scotia,
B3H 3A6, Can. Illustrates many quilts from Nova Scotia.
Examples are selected to illustrate points of design and
color rather than history. Available from the above address.

620. Made in Mississippi: Black Folk Art and Crafts.
Film, 20 min., color, sound, 1975. Artists talk about their
work in sculpture, quilting, painting and basketmaking. All
are black folk artists. Distributor: Center for Southern
Folklore, 1216 Peabody Ave., Box 40105, Memphis, Tenn.
38104. Director: Bill Ferris. Producer: Yale Media Design Studio in cooperation with the Center for Southern Folklore.

621. Missing Pieces: Contemporary Georgia Folk Art.
Film, 28 min., color, sound, 1976. Shows nineteenth-
century Georgia folk art, including the two Harriet Powers'
pictorial quilts. Followed by contemporary Georgia folk
artists and their work. Distributor: Odyssey Productions,
123 Northwest Second Ave., Portland, Ore. 97209. Director:
Steve Heiser. Producer: Odyssey Productions for the Georgia Council for the Arts and Humanities.

622. Molas Technique.
Forty-three slides. Demonstration by Elsie Blaschke of
RITES: 1980. Silk appliqué and stitchery. Available from:
Ontario Crafts Council, 346 Dundas St. W., Toronto, Ont.
M5T 1G5, Can.

623. The New American Quilt.
Slide Kit M5. Forty-one slides of contemporary quilts from
the exhibition held at the Museum of Contemporary Crafts
in 1976. Shows the work of twenty-five American artists.
Available from: American Crafts Council, 44 West 53rd
St., New York, N. Y. 10019.

624. Old Quilts in North Dakota.
Sixty-five slides. Shows antique quilts from each county.
Accompanying script discusses design and history of each
quilt. There are some full-size patterns. Available from:
Jane W. Winge, Clothing and Textiles Specialist, Cooperative
Extension Service, North Dakota State University, Fargo,
N. D. 58102.

625. Patchwork and Quilting.
Kit: Two cassettes, twelve spirit masters, two wall charts,
one teacher's guide. Discusses the design and technique of
patchwork. Encourages the student to use his own creativity.
Includes interviews with quilters and examples of their work.
Available from: Butterick Publishing, The Butterick Crafts
Program, 708 Third Avenue, New York, N. Y. 10017.

626. Patchwork Quilts.
        Film, 10 min.   Film on the quilt show Tradition Plus One:
        Patchwork Quilts from South Eastern Ontario, held in 1974
        at the Agnes Etherington Art Centre.   Directed by Kim
        Ondaatje.   Produced by Quarry Films, 1974.   Available
        from: Art Gallery of Ontario, Extension Dept., Grange
        Park, Toronto, Ont. M5T 1G4, Can.

627. Pioneer Living: Education and Recreation.
        Film, 11 min., color, sound, 1971.   Shows a quilting bee.
        Distributor: Coronet Instructional Media, 65 East South
        Water St., Chicago, Ill.   60601.   Producer: Moreland-
        Latchford Productions.

628. Quilt Fever.
        Thirteen-week series on MPBN-TV, Orono, Maine.   Shows
        quilts from the state of Maine.   Includes interview with
        Jeffrey Gutcheon.   Available from: Maine Public Broad-
        casting Network, Alumni Hall, University of Maine, Orono,
        Me.   04469.

629. Quilt National '83.
        Slide kit.   Shows quilts from the show.   Available from:
        American Crafts Council, 44 West 53rd St., New York,
        N. Y.   10019.

630. Quilt Toronto '81.
        108 slides.   Shows quilts from the show of the same name.
        Ontario Crafts Council, 346 Dundas St. W., Toronto, Ont.
        M5T 1G5, Can.

631. Quilted Works.
        Thirty-eight slides.   Ontario Crafts Council, 346 Dundas St.
        W., Toronto, Ont. M5T 1G5, Can.

632. Quilter's Holiday.
        Video Cassette.   Directed by Mercedes Maharis, P.O. Box
        1678, Santa Monica, Calif.   90406-1678.   This is a docu-
        mentary on annual quilting shows.   Presents criteria judges
        use to evaluate a quilt.   Looks at quilts, their makers and
        their construction.   Accompanied by music.

633. Quilting I.
        Thirteen-week series on PBS.   Produced by station WBGU-
        TV, Bowling Green, Ohio   43403.   Bowling Green State
        University.   Features Penny McMorris, Michael James,
        Nancy Crow and others.   Viewers' guides accompany each
        series.

634. Quilting II.
        Thirteen half-hour video-tape programs.   WBGU-TV, Bowl-
        ing Green, Ohio.   Covers Quilt National '81 and demonstra-
        tions with Michael James, Judi Warren, Darwin Bearly,

Nancy Crow, Florence Pulford, Edward Larson, Jinny Beyer,
Elizabeth Akana, Cuesta Benberry and Yvonne Porcella.

635.   Quilting Bee.
            Film, color, 11 min., sound.   Public is invited to join a
            quilting bee during their lunch hour.   Distributor/Producer:
            Resource Center, Crafts Council of Australia, 27 King St.,
            Sydney, Australia.

636.   Quilting: Patterns of Love.
            20 min., color, narrated, 16mm.   The audience meets
            quilters, both young and old.   Shows how quilts reflect the
            social times of their makers.   Traces the historical progress
            of quilting.   Produced by Larron Productions Ltd.   Available
            from: Cinema Concepts International 56 Shaftsbury Ave.,
            Toronto, Ont. M4T 1A3.

637.   Quilting Women.
            Film, 27 min., color, sound, 16mm, 1976.   Follows making
            a quilt from beginning to end.   Women talk about patterns
            and what they put into the quilt.   Accompanied by music.
            Distributor/Producer: Appalshop, Box 743, Whitesburg, Ky.
            41858.   Director: Elizabeth Barrett.

638.   Quilts: A Tradition in Southern Illinois.
            Slide/tape show illustrating the development of the exhibition
            of the same name and photos of many of the quilters.   No
            sound.   Available from: Chicago Public Library Cultural
            Center, Exhibit Hall, 78 East Washington St., Chicago, Ill.
            60602.

639.   Quilts by Judith Dingle.
            Forty slides.   Contemporary work by the artist.   1980.
            Ontario Crafts Council, 346 Dundas St. W., Toronto, Ont.
            M5T 1G5, Can.

640.   Quilts in Women's Lives.
            Film, 28 min., color, sound, 16mm, 1979.   Produced by
            Ferrero Films, 908 Rhode Island St., San Francisco, Calif.
            94107.   Made for the exhibit: American Quilts: A Handmade
            Legacy, held in Oakland, California.   Seven women talk
            about quiltmaking and what it means to them.   Also shows
            traditional quilt patterns.   Available in Canada: Mobius In-
            ternational, 100 Adelaide St. W., Ste. 408, Toronto, Ont.
            M5H 1S3, Can.

641.   Saint Louis Art Museum Resource Center.
            Educational packet of quilt slides (includes most of the pieces
            from the exhibition Take Cover.)   Forest Park, Saint Louis,
            Mo. 63110.

642.   Snyder, Grace McCance.
            Color slides.   Set 401: Eight Snyder Quilts 1932-1943,

twenty slides.   Set 609:   Seven Snyder Quilts 1944-1953,
twenty slides.   Available from: The Quilt Lady, Box 1166,
Grand Island, Neb.   68802.

643. Stitchery.
       Film, 15 min., color, 1969.   AIMS.   Instructional Media
       Services, 626 Justin Ave., Glendale, Calif.   91261.   Looks
       at technique used in embroidery, needlepoint and appliqué.
       Shows various designs for each.

644. Stitchery and Appliqué.
       Twenty slides.   Shows these two techniques.   Ontario Crafts
       Council, 346 Dundas St. W., Toronto, Ont. M5T 1G5, Can.

645. Surveys of American Crafts and Folk Arts from the Index of
       American Design (Textiles).
       National Gallery of Art, Washington, D. C.   20565.   Cat.
       #029.   Eighteen slides, cassette, 25 min. with text.   Shows
       textiles made in the home and early mills.   Contains a few
       quilts.

646. The Three Dreams of Grace McCance Snyder.
       Film, 13 min., sixty-three slides with thirty-five quilt slides.
       From: The Quilt Lady, Box 1166, Grand Island, Neb.
       68802.   Life story of Grace McCance Snyder.

647. Traditional Quilts from the Collection of Kim Ondaatje.
       Thirty-five slides, 1979.   Both appliquéd and pieced quilts
       from her collection.   Ontario Crafts Council, 346 Dundas
       St. W., Toronto, Ont. M5T 1G5, Can.

648. Under the Covers.
       Film, 11 min., color, sound, 16mm, narrated, 1976.   Writ-
       ten, directed and produced by Millie Paul.   Shows quilts
       from the Denver Art Museum, the Mollie Brown House, the
       Midwest and Pennsylvania.   Available from University of
       Illinois, University of Minnesota, Boston University and in
       Canada from International Tele Film Enterprises, 47 Densley
       St., Toronto, Ont., Can.   Distributor: Pyramid Films,
       M. P. Productions, 906 9th St., Santa Monica, Calif.   90403.

V. MUSEUM COLLECTIONS

649. Abby Aldrich Rockefeller Folk Art Center.
307 S. England St., Williamsburg, Va. 23185 (Tel. 804-229-1000) (Mailing address: P. O. Box C). Anne Watkins, Registrar. Collection contains over thirty quilts and quilt squares. There is no catalog.

650. Acadian Museum.
Champlain Bldg., Univ. of Moncton, Moncton, New Brunswick, E1A 3E9, Can. (Tel. 506-858-4082). Deborah Robichaud, curator. Small collection of three quilts: Log Cabin, Queen Victoria commemorative quilt, Puff quilt made from souvenir flags.

651. American Museum in Britain.
Claverton Manor, Bath, Avon, BA2 7BD, Eng. (Tel. 0225-60503). Sheila Betterton, Textile & Needlework Specialist. Museum opened in 1961 as a textile gallery with examples of whole cloth, pieced, appliquéd, crazy, candlewick, embroidered and trapunto bed covers covering the years from the mid-eighteenth century to the present. The book by Sheila Betterton entitled, Quilts and Coverlets from the American Museum illustrates about seventy-five quilts as well as candlewick and woven coverlets from the collection. The museum also has postcards and slides of quilts. They accept dollar cheques.

652. Art Institute of Chicago.
Michigan Ave. at Adams St., Chicago, Ill. 60603 (Tel. 313-433-3600). Cynthia J. Cannon, assistant to the curator, Dept. of Textiles. The institute is now compiling slide kits based on the permanent holdings. There is no set date for its release. Catalog documenting the collection: American Quilts from the Art Institute of Chicago, 1966, by Mildred Davison.

653. Atlanta Historical Society.
3101 Andrews Drive, N. W., Atlanta, Ga. 30305 (P. O. Box 12423). Cady Bissell Ferguson, director of public relations (Tel. 404-261-1837). Collection documented in Southern Comfort: Quilts from the Atlanta Historical Society Collection, 1978.

654. Baltimore Museum of Art.

Art Museum Drive, Baltimore, Md.   21218 (Tel. 301-396-
7100).   Dena S. Katzenberg, consultant curator of textiles.
Noted for its collection of album quilts.   These have been
documented by Dena Katzenberg's Baltimore Album Quilts,
1981.   124pp.

655.   Bernice P. Bishop Museum.
       1344 Kalihi St., Honolulu, Hawaii 96818 (P.O. Box 19000-A)
       (Tel. 808-847-3511).   Betty L. Long, curatorial assistant.
       No documentation of a small collection of six Hawaiian quilts,
       four of which are flag quilts.   Examples: Pineapple Design,
       cotton; Hawaiian Flag Quilt, cotton.

656.   British Columbia Provincial Museum.
       675 Belleville St., Victoria, British Columbia V8V 1X4,
       Can. (Tel. 604-387-3014).   Zane H. Lewis, curator of so-
       cial history.   The collection is documented on catalog cards.
       There are no catalogs or slides available.   Examples: Star
       of Bethlehem; Grandmother's Flower Garden, 1980; Log
       Cabin, 1930's and Basket pattern, Ontario, c. 1890.

657.   Brooklyn Museum.
       188 Eastern Pkwy., Brooklyn, N. Y.   11238 (Tel. 212-638-
       5000).   Carol Krute, curatorial assistant.   The museum has
       a large collection, well documented with slides and photo-
       graphs.   There are 154 quilts dating from 1790 through the
       early twentieth century.   E. g., pieced chintz, 1775; Dia-
       monds on red background, 1930 and Star crib quilt, mid-
       nineteenth century.

658.   Canadian Centre for Folk Culture Studies.   National Museum
       of Man.
       Metcalfe & McLeod Streets, Ottawa, Ont. K1A 0M8, Can.
       (Tel. 613-992-3497).   Now has custody of the main portion
       of the quilt collection of the National Museum of Man.

659.   Cincinnati Art Museum.
       Eden Park, Cincinnati, Ohio   45202 (Tel. 513-721-5204).
       Carolyn R. Shine, curator, costumes, textiles, tribal arts.
       There is no published catalog of their collection.   Many of
       the museum's quilts have appeared in America's Quilts and
       Coverlets, by Safford and Bishop.   New Discoveries in Amer-
       ican Quilts, by Robert Bishop.   Quilts in America, by Patsy
       and Myron Orlofsky.

660.   Cleveland Museum of Art.
       11150 East Blvd. at University Circle, Cleveland, Ohio
       44106 (Tel. 216-421-7340).   Mr. Delbert R. Gutridge, reg-
       istrar.   The Department of Textiles has only one quilt,
       dated 1857.   This is pictured on p. 335 of Adelaide Hecht-
       linger's American Quilts, Quilting & Patchwork....   The
       extension division has three American quilts: 1.   Star of
       Bethlehem, late nineteenth century; 2.   Floral appliqué, late
       nineteenth century, Pennsylvania and 3.   Checkerboard, with

embroidered flowers, twentieth century, Mississippi. The
museum has photographs of its quilts, through the registrar.

661. Colorado Historical Society.
One Colorado Heritage Center, 1300 Broadway, Denver,
Colo. 80203. (Tel. 303-866-3682). Susan Gillis, assistant
curator of material culture. This fairly large collection has
been catalogued and the society has slides on each. There
is no published catalog nor can the slides be borrowed or
purchased.

662. Confederation Centre of the Arts.
Charlottetown, P. O. Box 848, Richmond St. , Prince Edward
Island C1A 7L9, Can. (Tel. 902-892-2464). Mark B. Holton,
curator. Seven quilts in the collection. Slides and photographs available from the registrar, Mrs. Judy MacDonald.
The museum acquired some items photographed in the exhibition catalog, Sunshine and Shadow, for its permanent
collection. Examples: The E. P. A. Quilt, 1978; Scenic
Drives of P. E. I. , 1977-78; St. Peters Road.

663. Cortland County Historical Society Inc.
25 Homer Ave. , Cortland, N. Y. 13045 (Tel. 607-756-
6071). Leslie C. O'Malley, director. Thirty-five quilts
in the collection, most made between 1850 and 1900, rep-
resenting typical quilts from that period. At present there
are no slides or catalogs. The museum is planning a major
textile exhibit in 1984 and will have both a catalog and slides
available at that time. Scholars may study the collection
by appointment.

664. D. A. R. Museum.
1776 D Street, N. E. , Washington, D. C. 20006-5392 (Tel.
202-628-1776). Libbie Heck, assistant registrar. Sixty-
one slides available for rent or purchase. The quilt collection numbers over 200 quilts and coverlets. There are
examples of whole cloth and whitework, stuffed work, pieced,
Log Cabin, Pineapple, baby quilt, appliqué, reverse appliqué,
album, crazy and silk quilts from the eighteenth and nineteenth centuries. The slides have an accompanying script.
Documented by the catalog American Quilts: 1780-1880,
1982, 12pp.

665. Denver Art Museum.
100 West 14th Ave. Parkway, Denver, Colo. 80204 (Tel.
303-575-2793). The museum now has 300 examples. It
includes thirty-five Charlotte Whitehall quilts. The collection has been documented by the following catalogs: Quilt
Collection (1963), by Lydia R. Dunham and Quilts and Coverlets (1974), by Imelda DeGraw.

666. Detroit Historical Museum.
54091 Woodward Ave. , Detroit, Mich. 48202 (Tel. 313-833-
1805). Cynthia Young, curator, social history division.

There has been no catalog documentation of the collection.
One of the museum's quilts appeared in Quilts '82, the Main
Street Press Calendar; Warner's Collector's Guide to American Quilts, 1981 and the catalog World of Quilts at Meadowbrook Hall features one of their quilts.

667. Edmonton, Alberta, City Artifacts Center.
      104th Avenue, c/o 10th Floor CN Tower, Edmonton, Alb.
      T5J 0K1 (Tel. 403-432-0644). William Steil, acting curator.
      Holds quilts previously housed in Fort Edmonton Park and
      the John Walter Museum. Two of these quilts were featured
      in Mary Conroy's book Canada Quilts. Quilts at the Arti-
      facts Center are documented in a card catalog with descrip-
      tion and historical information.

668. Esprit de Corps.
      900 Minnesota Street, San Francisco, Calif. 94107 (Tel.
      415-648-6900). Doug Tomkins, owner. Over 100 antique
      quilts dating from 1800-1940, noted for their color and graphic
      design. Articles on the collection published in Quilter's
      Newsletter, May 1982, pp. 12-14. Six quilts photographed
      in color in the Quilt Digest, 1983 by Michael Kile, pp. 56-
      61. Seven color photos. Tours arranged by appointment.

669. Essex Institute.
      132 Essex St., Salem, Mass. 01970 (Tel. 617-744-3390).
      Anne Farnum, curator. No published documentation at this
      time. Quilt collection numbers about twenty-five with a num-
      ber of good examples of crazy quilts from the 1870's. The
      cotton quilt collection dates to the mid-nineteenth century.

670. Glenbow Museum. Glenbow-Alberta Institute.
      130 Ninth Ave. S.E., Calgary, Alberta T2G 0P3, Can. (Tel.
      403-264-8300). Frances Roback assistant curator. Eighty
      quilts in the Cultural History Dept. of the Museum. No
      books or catalogs on the collection. Most of these quilts
      are documented by slides and/or photos. The museum does
      have some history on each individual quilt. Slides and photos
      are available for a fee, but are not of publishable quality.

671. Helen Foresman Spencer Museum of Art.
      University of Kansas, Lawrence, Kan. (Tel. 913-864-4710).
      Janet Dreiling, registrar. There are over 200 quilts in the
      collection, documented in the following catalogs: 150 Years
      of American Quilts, (1973), now O.P. Lea Rosson in an
      article in 104 Antiques pp. 102-5, December 1973. The
      foundation of the collection began in 1928 with a bequest by
      Mrs. William B. Thayer of fifty-three quilts made before
      1920. This was followed by the Hall and Kretsinger collec-
      tions. The Malcom-James collection was presented in 1972.
      It also holds the Carrie Hall quilt block collection. Six
      James quilts are from the first part of this century.

672. Henry Ford Museum & Greenfield Village.
      P.O. Box 1970, Dearborn, Mich.   48121 (Tel. 313-271-
      1620). Nancy V. Bryk, assistant curator of textiles. The
      museum has no documentation of its collection. Detail of
      linen bed cover embroidered in wool (1740) in Nina Holland
      Pictorial Quilting, p. 78; Buffalo Bill appliquéd quilt (1880),
      Pennsylvania, p. 97.

673. Historical Society of Delaware.
      505 Market Street Mall, Wilmington, Del.   19801 (Tel. 302-
      655-7161). Rebecca J. Hammell, museum curator. The
      museum contains six quilts, documented on catalog cards.
      There are no books, photos or slides. Example: Flying
      Geese (c. 1850-1899). The society has 8" x 10" black-and-
      white glossies and slides for which they charge a fee.

674. Honolulu Academy of Art.
      900 S. Beretania Street, Honolulu, Hawaii 96814 (Tel. 808-
      538-3693). Sanna Saks Deutsch, registrar. The academy
      holds thirty-five quilts from the mainland, most from the
      second half of the nineteenth century. Also has represen-
      tations from Pennsylvania and the Midwest with several
      Amish examples. Holds twenty Hawaiian quilts, most made
      prior to 1918. Many were shown in the exhibition Hawaiian
      Quilts in 1973 for which there was a catalog.

675. Hudson River Museum, Trevor Park-on-Hudson.
      511 Warburton Ave., Yonkers, N. Y.   10701 (Tel. 914-963-
      4550). Margi Conrads, research curator. Collection con-
      sists of eighteen cotton patchwork quilts and crazy quilts
      from the late-nineteenth and early-twentieth centuries. There
      is no published documentation.

676. Illinois State Museum.
      Spring & Edwards Streets, Springfield, Ill. 62706 (Tel. 217-
      782-7386). Lowell E. Anderson, decorative arts curator.
      Collection numbers sixty-two quilts, most of which are docu-
      mented on slides. There is no catalog of the collection.

677. Kamloops Museum Assn.
      207 Seymour St., Kamloops, British Columbia V2C 2E7, Can.
      John Stewart, Asst. Archivist (Tel. 604-372-9931). Collection
      consists of five quilts donated by families in the Kamloops
      area, although not all necessarily made there. E.g., Log
      Cabin (c. 1900); two red-and-white patchwork squares (c.
      1870); Patchwork quilt (c. 1935); patchwork quilt (c. 1890's);
      white quilt (c. 1909) with names embroidered of those who
      attended the Methodist Regional Convention in Kamloops on
      April 13, 1909.

678. Kentucky Historical Museum.
      200 Broadway, Frankfort, Ky.   40601, P.O. Box H (Tel.
      502-564-3016). Catherine P. Zwyer, collections manager.

Collection documented by registration cards with black-and-white photos and some slides. There is no catalog at this time.

679. Levan's Hall.
Kendall, Cumbria, Eng. LA8 0PB (Tel. 0448-6032). Mrs. Margaret Lambert, secretary. This is not a museum. However, it contains what is thought to be the earliest known patchwork in England. A quilt made in 1708 from Indian printed cottons.

680. Library of Congress.
American Folklife Center. Archive of Folk Culture, Washington, D. C. 20540. Joseph C. Hickerson, head, Archive of Folk Culture (Tel. 202-287-5000). No quilt collection. The archive does have field slides recordings and some slides of quilts and quiltmaking. Tapes and slides may be copied but it is time consuming and expensive, requiring the user to do firsthand research at the library to identify his/her needs.

681. Louisiana State Museum.
751 Chartres St., New Orleans, La. 70116, P. O. Box 2458 (Tel. 504-568-6968). Maud Margaret Lyon, curator of costumes and textiles. There is no catalog available. The collection numbers about forty quilts. Collection consists of quilts made or used in Louisiana. The staff dates the quilts by fabric. They do not have a history of each quilt. The museum has recently acquired three quilts from Melrose Plantation and one from Houma, Louisiana. These later acquisitions are better documented.

682. Lyman Allyn Museum.
100 Mohegan Ave. (625 Williams St.), New London, Conn. 06320 (Tel. 203-443-2545). Ten quilts in the collection. There are slides, black-and-white photos, 8" x 10" and 4" x 5" color transparencies. E. g., pieced quilt (c. 1875) from New York, stenciled Rose (c. 1850), satin patchwork (1890), reversible wool and cotton (c. 1830) and Star design (c. 1860).

683. McCord Museum.
690 Sherbrooke St. West, McGill University, Montreal, Quebec H3A 1E9, Can. (Tel. 514-392-4778). Mrs. Jacqueline Beaudoin-Ross, curator, costumes & textiles. Collection of about forty quilts, mostly all Canadian. They are cataloged on cards. Museum has slides of about six of these available for a fee. The collection may be used for research but by appointment only. One quilt is documented in "An Early Eighteenth Century Pieced Quilt in Montreal" 6#2 Canadian Art Review by Mrs. Beaudoin-Ross.

684. Manchester City Art Galleries.

Mosley Street, Manchester, Lancastershire NRI 3JU (Tel.
061-2369422). Jane Tozer, keeper. The Museum of Costume no longer collects textiles, but has retained those few
collected before the war. They have five quilts and one
embroidered bedcover. The collection dates from the early
eighteenth through the nineteenth centuries. Their best
example is a block quilt embroidered with the name Elizabeth Jefferson, 1811. This has been pictured in Patchwork
by Avril Colby, plate 123.

685. Manitoba Museum of Man & Nature.
190 Rupert Ave., Winnipeg, Manitoba R3B 0N2, Can. (Tel.
204-956-2830). Catherine Collins, chief conservator. There
is no documentation in book form. Over twelve quilts in
the collection. Some history is known for these. They are
documented with cards and photos. E.g., 1. Squares
(early twentieth century, Manitoba); 2. Tulip appliqué (1890,
Ontario); 3. signature quilt; 4. silk patchwork; 5. Pineapple (Ontario), mid-nineteenth century; 6. crazy; 7. crazy
(c. 1880), Ontario and 8. Star pattern (Ontario).

686. Massillon Museum.
212 Lincoln Way East, Massillon, Ohio 44646 (Tel. 216-833-
4061). Margy Vogt, registrar. There is no complete documentation of the collection, except their catalog cards. The
collection consists of twenty-eight quilts. E.g., crazy; Rose
of Sharon; pieced silk; commemorative name quilt (1851-
1898); appliqué; Blazing Star; Barn Raising; Log Cabin (c.
1880) and Appliqué of Four Eagles (c. 1850).

687. Metropolitan Museum of Art.
Fifth Avenue at 82nd St., New York, N. Y. 10028 (Tel.
212-535-7710). Documented in the catalog by Marilyn Bordes,
12 Great Quilts from the American Wing, 1974, 36pp. Examples from the nineteenth and twentieth centuries, illustrating various techniques. Includes the Phoebe Warner Coverlet (c. 1800).

688. Minnesota Historical Society.
1500 Mississippi St., St. Paul, Minn. 55101 (Tel. 612-296-
6980). Marcia Anderson, curator of collections. Museum:
690 Cedar St.; Research Center: 1500 Mississippi St. Collection consists of between 150 and 200 quilts, patchwork and
appliqué, illustrating many patterns from the early nineteenth
century to the present. The museum completed a project in
1982 to photograph all the quilts in the collection. They now
have color and black-and-white photos of each quilt. The
collection is documented in the exhibition catalog entitled,
Minnesota Patchwork, 1979 and the article "Minnesota Patchwork" by Nicholas Westbrook and Carolyn Gilman in Minnesota History (Summer 1979), pp. 237-245.

689. Mississippi State Historical Museum.

North State & Capitol Streets, P.O. Box 571, Jackson,
Miss.   39205 (Tel. 601-354-6222).   Mary Bohrenz, curator
of collections.   Many of their quilts' histories are recorded
from recollections of the donors.   Twenty-eight of the quilts
were shown in an exhibition in 1976.   However, there was
no catalog for this show.   Examples of some of these quilts:
puff pattern, twentieth century; 1972 appliqué of Choctaw
Indian Girls and Tepees; Sawtooth (c. 1862); Rocky Mountain
(c. 1860); Tree of Life (1930's); Broken Circle (c. 1905)
and Pineapple (1870).   Color slides are available for most
of these quilts for a fee.

690.   Museum of American Folk Art.
       49 West 53rd St., New York, N. Y.   10019 (Tel. 212-581-
       2474).   Joyce Hill, curator.   Important recent acquisitions
       are the David Pottinger gift in 1981 of fifteen Midwestern
       Amish crib quilts; also his collection of quilts from the Elk-
       hart and LaGrange Counties in Indiana that date from 1870-
       1940, including Fan, Bow Tie, Lone Star and Hole in the
       Barn Door.   These have been documented in the catalog
       Quilts from the Indiana Amish by David Pottinger.

691.   Museum of Fine Arts, Boston.
       465 Huntington Ave., Boston, Mass.   02115 (Tel. 617-267-
       9300).   Catherine K. Hunter, acting curator, textiles & cos-
       tumes.   Collection numbers about thirty quilts, including the
       pictorial quilt by Harriet Powers.   A slide set with details
       of the quilt is available from the slide library of the mu-
       seum.

692.   National Gallery of Art.
       Consititution Ave. at 6th St., Washington, D. C.   20565
       (Tel. 202-737-4215).   Caroline H. Backlund, head, reader
       services.   Houses the Index of American Design, a Federal
       Art Project that was part of the Works Progress Adminis-
       tration.   There are 22, 000 drawings and photographs with
       information sheets portraying American decorative art, in-
       cluding quilts from the time of settlement to about 1900.
       It covered each state and ran from 1935-1942.   The collec-
       tion is open to the public for study purposes.   Also avail-
       able on microfilm.

693.   National Museum of American History--Division of Textiles,
       Smithsonian Institution.
       14th St. & Constitution Ave. N. W., Washington, D. C.
       20560 (Tel. 202-357-1300).   Collection began in the 1890's
       with a gift of three late-eighteenth- and early-nineteenth-
       century quilts.   It now comprises about 300 quilts and un-
       quilted tops, small pieces and sections.   Overview of most
       of the techniques used in the quilts for these dates.   The
       museum has photographs and color slides available for sixty-
       nine of these quilts for a fee.   There are also some detail
       pictures.   Annotations include maker's name, date and locale,

where known.   E. g., Rose of Sharon (c. 1860), Hexagon
pieced quilt (c. 1830), Floral appliqué (1849), Double Irish
Chain (1825-30), Star of Bethlehem (c. 1880); slides of the
Harriet Powers Bible Quilt (c. 1886) and 4" x 5" color
transparency and black-and-white photos, including description of each block by the artist and the purchaser.

694.   The New Brunswick Museum.
277 Douglas Ave., St. John, New Brunswick E2K 1E5, Can.
(Tel. 506-693-1196).   Valerie Simpson, assistant curator of
decorative arts.   There is no published documentation of the
collection.   The museum has between twenty-five and fifty
quilts, mostly appliquéd.   Their best and most well-known
quilt is the "Mary Morton" named after its maker.   It is
all white linen pieced of three strips, with a diamond quilted
center and dates from 1760-1770.

695.   New York State Historical Assn.
Fenimore House, Lake Road, Cooperstown, N. Y.   13326
(Tel. 607-547-2533).   Ronald Burch, registrar.   Collection
has not yet been photographed on color slides.   Fourteen
of their quilts are photographed in black and white.   These
are available in Xerox copies for study use only, for a fee.
The collection has been documented in a thesis by Katheryn
Thomas entitled, Quilts in the New York State Historical
Association's Collection, 1977, 162pp.

696.   Newark Museum.
49 Washington St., Newark, N. J.   07101 (Tel. 201-733-
6600).   Phillip Curtis, curator.   The first quilt exhibit was
held in 1914.   In 1918 the museum began its permanent collection.   Shows thereafter were held in 1920, 1927, 1929,
1943 and 1947.   The collection increased to over fifty quilts,
with shows in 1950, 1960, 1961 and 1965, as related by Phillip Curtis in his catalog.   The Optical Quilts Exhibit was
the first show by a major museum emphasizing the abstract
design of quilts.   The collection now numbers over 100 examples dating from the early eighteenth century to the 1940's.
Published documentation includes Quilts and Counterpanes in
the Newark Museum, 1948 by Margaret White and American
Quilts in the Newark Museum Collection, 1973 by Phillip
Curtis.

697.   North Carolina Museum of History.
109 East James St., Raleigh, N. C. 27611 (Tel. 919-733-
3894).   Martha E. Battle, assistant registrar.   There are
about eighty quilts in the collection, mostly pieced and appliquéd.   The earliest dates from about 1800, and nearly all
are from North Carolina.   Examples from the collection:
Double Sawtooth Variation, Irish Chain, Log Cabin (c. 1925)
and (1907), Rose Tree (c. 1850) and Sunburst (c. 1880).

698.   Nova Scotia Museum Complex.

1747 Summer St., Halifax, Nova Scotia B3H 3A6 (Tel. 902-
429-4610). Scott Robson, curator, historic buildings & fur-
nishings. They have a good collection of local quilts. Some
quilts from the collection are illustrated in Nova Scotia Patchwork Patterns, 1981 by Carter Houck and 300 Years of Canada's Quilts, 1976 by Mary Conroy. The curator has prepared a slide tape lecture entitled, "Looking at Quilts."
It consists of sixty-three slides illustrating many quilts in
Nova Scotia. Its emphasis is on design and color rather
than history. This lecture can be borrowed by writing to
"Education Loans" at the above address.

699. Oklahoma Historical Society.
      State Museum Historical Bldg., Oklahoma City, Okla. 73105-
      4997 (Tel. 405-521-2491). John R. Hill, curator. The col-
      lection has been documented in A Century of Quilts from the
      Oklahoma Historical Society. This catalog illustrates exam-
      ples of each type of quilt in the collection and the 1981 show.
      There has been no significant addition to the collection since
      that time. There are other quilts held by the ten additional
      museums within the Oklahoma Historical Society. The state
      collection as of 1982 numbered ninety-seven.

700. Peale Museum.
      225 Holliday St., Baltimore, Md. 21202 (Tel. 301-396-
      3523). Dean Krimmel, supervisor, Museum Reference
      Center. The collection consists of six quilts. Four or
      five are patchwork from about 1845-1920's. There is also
      an appliquéd Friendship quilt (c. 1845) that appears in Saf-
      ford & Bishop's America's Quilts & Coverlets, p. 206, 1972.

701. Pennsylvania Farm Museum of Landis Valley.
      2451 Kissel Hill Rd., Lancaster, Pa. 17120 (Tel. 717-
      569-0401). Vernon S. Gunnion, curator of collections. The
      collection is catalogued but without pictures. Most of their
      specimens are full-size with a few crib quilts.

702. Philadelphia Museum of Art.
      26th & Benjamin Franklin Pkwy., Box 7646, Philadelphia,
      Pa. 19101-7647 (Tel. 215-763-8100). Susan Anderson,
      assistant curator, costumes and textiles. The museum has
      a large collection of about 250 quilts. There are examples
      of eighteenth-century Philadelphia quilts and Pennsylvania
      German examples. These have been documented in The
      Pennsylvania German Collection, 1982 by Beatrice Garvin,
      pp. 263-265.

703. Royal Ontario Museum.
      100 Queen's Park, Toronto, Ont. M5S 2C6, Can. (Tel. 416-
      978-3655). Mrs. Greta Ferguson, Textile Dept. There
      has been no documentation since the 1975 catalog Pieced
      Quilts of Ontario, by Dorothy Burnham. The entire collec-
      tion consists of about 159 quilts, the majority of which are

Canadian with a few American and some English examples.
The museum has about fifty slides that can be duplicated
for a fee. Since 1964, the museum has housed the collection from the Quebec Branch of the Canadian Craft Guild
of Montreal.

704. Royal Scottish Museum.
Chambers Street, Edinburgh, Scotland EH1 1JF (Tel. 431-
225-7534). Naomi Tarrant, curator of European costume
& textiles. The collection consists of ten patchwork pieces,
some quilted, and ten that are "blind quilted" and embroidered. None have been made into postcards or slides, nor
have they been documented in a catalog or book.

705. San Antonio Museum Association.
3801 Broadway, Brackenridge Park, P.O. Box 2601, San
Antonio, Tex. 78209 (Tel. 512-226-5544). Jane Parker
Hagino, administrative assistant, Textile Dept. The association has a card catalog with information on each quilt
such as size, technique, date and provenance. There are
150 quilts in the collection with one or two data cards on
each. There is a charge for postage and photocopying of
cards. There is no published documentation of the entire
quilt collection.

706. The Shelburne Museum.
Shelburne, Vt. 05482 (Tel. 802-985-3346). Polly Mitchell,
textile preparator. The collection consists of over 600
quilts and bedcovers of every type. They are all cataloged.
Photocopied information is available on all for a charge.
They have slides and black-and-white prints for purchase.
The quilts date from the late eighteenth century to the early
twentieth. The majority are from the nineteenth. The col-
lection has been documented in Pieced Work and Appliqué
Quilts at the Shelburn Museum, 1957 by Lilian B. Carlisle.
Now O.P. The museum hopes to have a new quilt book in
the near future.

707. Southern Illinois University.
American Studies Program. Folklore Archive, Edwardsville,
Ill. 62025 (Tel. 618-692-2000). John Oldani, director.
No films or slides in the archive. University does have
thousands of quilt patterns which are available to the public
for a nominal fee. Although there is no catalog or books,
the archive does have a partial listing of its contents.

708. Southern Oregon Historical Society.
Jacksonville Oregon Museum. 206 North Fifth St., Jacksonville, Ore. 97530 (Tel. 503-899-1847). Gregory A. Gault-
ieri, registrar of collections. There is no documentation
in the form of a book, catalog or museum bulletin article.
The museum has slides of quilts done by local museum
quilters (hand sewn and quilted). For the cost per slide,

contact Mr. Richard Engeman. There are over 100 quilts
photographed and cataloged on 5'' x 8'' cards. The museum
will send copies of cards for a fee.

709.   Stamford Historical Society Inc.
       713 Bedford St., Stamford, Conn. 06901 (Tel. 203-323-
       1975). Mrs. Alfred W. Dater, Jr., curator. The museum
       has a collection of thirty-two quilts documented as being
       made in Stamford, Connecticut. They have examples of
       six appliqué, two candlewick and embroidery, four crazy,
       five crib, two linsey-woolsey, twelve patchwork, and one
       trapunto whitework. Some of their quilts were featured in
       Ladies Circle Needlework, Winter 1973, pp. 20-23; America's
       Quilts and Coverlets by Safford and Bishop and in Patchwork
       and Quilts by Barbara von Roemer, Switzerland, 1982, pp.
       194 & 195.

710.   Ulster Folk and Transport Museum.
       Cultra Manor, Holywood County Down, Northern Ireland
       (Tel. Holywood 5411). Mr. W. Craford, keeper of material
       culture. The Folk Museum has a collection of over 300
       quilts representing patchwork, appliqué and whole cloth.
       The bulk of the collection is from Belfast, County Antrim
       and County Down, with a few examples from Armagh, Lon-
       donderry and Fermanagh. Most date from the late nineteenth
       century, and some are documented with the maker's name
       and date. Some quilts from the collection were in the show
       Irish Bedcovers, a traveling exhibition in 1981-82. Most
       of the quilts in the museum's collection are on prints (8''
       x 10'' black and white) and color slides.

711.   Wadsworth Atheneum.
       600 Main St., Hartford, Conn. 06103 (Tel. 203-278-2670).
       Lynn Ritland, assistant to the curator, costumes & textiles.
       One of their quilts is photographed and annotated in Quilts
       in America by Patsy and Myron Orlofsky.

712.   The Welsh Folk Museum.
       St. Fagans, Cardiff, Wales CF5 6XB (Tel. 0222-569441,
       Ext. 371). Ilid Anthony, curator. The museum has a good
       representative quilt collection. Most are patchwork, hexa-
       gon designs, Log Cabin, crazy and geometric designs. Strip
       quilting is not done in Wales. Quilting motifs include cir-
       cular dishes, flowers, central square or diamond and borders.
       They have black-and-white prints of a number of the quilts
       which are for sale. Ilid Anthony wrote an article describ-
       ing the collection in #12 Winter 1975 Amguedda: Bulletin
       of the National Museum of Wales. 15pp. "Quilting and
       Patchwork in Wales." Since this article, he has written
       another article which he hopes will be published soon.

713.   Western Reserve Historical Society.
       10825 East Blvd., Cleveland, Ohio 44106 (Tel. 216-721-5722).

Jairus B. Baines, director, History Museum. The society has an extensive quilt collection which has been catalogued on cards. However there are no slides.

714.   Winterthur Museum.
Winterthur, Del. 19735 (Tel. 302-656-8591). Mrs. Susan Swan, curator of textiles. Two books document the collection: Winterthur Guide to American Needlework and Plain and Fancy: American Women and Their Needlework, both by Susan Swan. There have been acquisitions since these books. Five in all. Some recently acquired: Star quilt (1837), pieced quilt top (c. 1800-1810) and autographed quilt (1845).

715.   Worthing Museum and Art Gallery.
Chapel Road, Worthing, West Sussex, Eng. BN11 1 HVQ (Tel. 0903-39999). The collection consists of about forty bedspreads, a small number of these are quilted patchwork. They were included in the exhibition Sew to Bed. An appointment is needed to see the quilt collection. Slides and postcards of the collection are available by special order. E. g. , patchwork (1860) and (1830-40), two patchwork quilts (1830) and patchwork bedspread (1840-50).

716.   Canada Quilts. 13 Pinewood Ave., Grimsby, Ont. L3M 1W2,
       Can. Published five times per year. News items, instruc-
       tions, patterns and photos.

717.   La Plata Review. La Plata Press, P. O. Box 820, Evans, Colo.
       80620. Published quarterly. Book reviews. October is-
       sues devoted to one particular subject such as quilt design
       or history.

718.   Ladies Circle Patchwork Quilts. Lopez Publications Inc., 21
       West 26th St., New York, N. Y. 10010. Published four
       times per year. Book reviews, patterns, color photos and
       features.

719.   Patchwork Magazine. Mc-Square Co. Ltd. 4-27-3 Daizawa,
       Setagaya-Ku, Tokyo 155, Japan. Published quarterly. For-
       merly known as the McSquare Quilt News. Color cover,
       color and black-and-white photos. Written in Japanese.
       Instructions, news items and biographical sketches. Avail-
       able to subscribers outside of Japan.

720.   Patchwork Patter. Quarterly publication of the National Quilt-
       ing Assn. Inc., P. O. Box 62, Greenbelt, Md. 20770. Quilt
       patterns, instructions, quilt show reviews and chapter and
       membership news. Comes with membership to association.

721.   Quilt. Harris Publications Inc., 79 Madison Ave., New York,
       N. Y. 10016. Published quarterly. Patterns, designs,
       instructions, feature articles and color photos.

722.   The Quilt Digest. Kiracofe & Kile, 955 14th Street, San Fran-
       cisco, Calif. 94114. A journal published annually. Color
       photos and articles by quilt researchers. Photos of antique
       and modern quilts.

723.   Quilt World. House of White Birches Inc., Box 337, Seabrook,
       N. H. 03874. Published bi-monthly. Began in 1976. Book
       reviews, features, patterns and color photos.

724.   Quilt World Christmas Annual. House of White Birches Inc.,
       P. O. Box 337, Seabrook, N. H. 03874. Published annually.
       Began 1977. Christmas patterns.

725.   Quilt World Omnibook.   P.O. Box 337, Seabrook N. H.   03874.
       Published four times per year.   Spring, summer, fall, win-
       ter.   Patterns, quilt designs, news, column news and fea-
       tures.

726.   Quilt World Omnibook Christmas Special.   House of White
       Birches Inc., P.O. Box 337, Seabrook, N. H.   03874.
       Many full-size Christmas patterns.

727.   Quilters Journal.   Box 270, Mill Valley, Calif.   94942.   His-
       tory of quilts and textiles.

728.   Quilter's Newsletter Magazine.   Leman Publications, 6700 W.
       44th Ave., Wheatridge, Colo.   80033.   Ten issues per year.
       News of forthcoming quilt shows, color photos of readers'
       quilts, regular features on "Old Time Quilting," modern
       quilting and quilting lessons.   Book reviews.

729.   Quiltmaker.   Dept. 5 P, Wheatridge, Colo.   80034.   Published
       two times per year by the editors of Quilter's Newsletter
       Magazine.   Pattern magazine, color illustrations and full-
       size patterns.

730.   Stitch 'n Sew Quilts.   Tower Press, P.O. Box 428, Seabrook,
       N. H.   03874.   Published bi-monthly.   Patterns, color
       photos, features.   Also published Christmas Annual.

ADDENDA

731. Influences: Traditional and Contemporary Quilts. Wheatridge,
Colo.: Leman Publications, 1983. 43 pp.
    Documents show held at the Helen Foresman Spencer Mu-
seum of Art from August 21 through October 16, 1983. Exhibit illustrates the influence of traditional quilt patterns on the work of
contemporary quilt artists. Introductions written by Barbara Brackman
and Chris Wolf Edmonds. Includes bibiographical sketch of each
artist and his/her personal statement. Thirty-five quilts photographed
in color, annotated with quilt name, maker (if known), locale, date,
fabric and technique, size and owner.

732. Kluser, Verena. Amerikanische Quilts 1870-1940. Krefeld,
West Germany: Museum Haus Esters, 1983. 46pp.
    Sixteen color photos of Amish quilts with pertinent in-
formation. Five black-and-white photos. Documents show of Amish
quilts held from September 4 through October 23, 1983 at the Museum
Haus Esters, Krefeld, West Germany. Includes footnotes and bibliography. Text written in German.

733. _____. Made in America: Quilts. Munich, West Germany:
Schellmann & Kluser, 1982. 37pp.
    Ten color photos. Eight black-and-white photos of quilts.
Documents quilt show at the Verena Kluser Gallery in October 1982.
Photos noted with quilt name, locale, year, fabric and size. Intro-
ductory text in German, with some black-and-white photos of the
Amish people.

INDEX